A LOT TO LEARN

# A LOT TO LEARN

*Girls, Women and Education in the 20th Century*

Helen Jefferson Lenskyj

Women's Press

Toronto

A Lot to Learn: Girls, Women and Education in the 20th Century
Helen Jefferson Lenskyj

First published in 2005 by
**Women's Press, an imprint of Canadian Scholars' Press Inc.**
180 Bloor Street West, Suite 801
Toronto, Ontario
M5S 2V6

www.womenspress.ca

Copyright © 2005 Helen Jefferson Lenskyj and Canadian Scholars' Press Inc. All rights reserved. No part of this publication may be photocopied, reproduced, stored in a retrieval system, or transmitted, in any form or by any means, electronic, mechanical, or otherwise, without the written permission of Canadian Scholars' Press, except for brief passages quoted for review purposes. In the case of photocopying, a licence may be obtained from Access Copyright: One Yonge Street, Suite 1900, Toronto, Ontario, M5E 1E5, (416) 868-1620, fax (416) 868-1621, toll-free 1-800-893-5777, www.accesscopyright.ca.

Every reasonable effort has been made to identify copyright holders. Women's Press would be pleased to have any errors or omissions brought to its attention.

Canadian Scholars' Press/Women's Press gratefully acknowledges financial support for our publishing activities from the Ontario Arts Council, the Canada Council for the Arts, and the Government of Canada through the Book Publishing Industry Development Program (BPIDP).

**Library and Archives Canada Cataloguing in Publication**

Lenskyj, Helen Jefferson, 1943–
    A lot to learn : girls, women and education in the 20th century / Helen Jefferson Lenskyj.

Includes bibliographical references.
ISBN 0-88961-448-2

    1. Girls—Australia—Education—History—20th century. 2. Women—Australia—Education—History—20th century. 3. Women's studies. 4. Lesbian teachers—Canada—Biography. 5. Lenskyj, Helen Jefferson, 1943– I. Title.

LC1762.L45 2005         371.822         C2004-906148-8

Cover design, text design and layout: Susan Thomas/Digital Zone

Front cover photo: The author, age five, in Kambala uniform, 1947 (author's collection).

05  06  07  08  09    5  4  3  2  1

Printed and bound in Canada by AGMV Marquis Imprimeur, Inc.

In loving memory of my mother, Margaret Jefferson,
and my mentor and friend, Mary O'Brien

# Table of Contents

Acknowledgments ................................................................................. ix

Introduction ............................................................................................ xi

**Introduction to Part I** ............................................................................ 1

CHAPTER 1  "... A Bad Start in My Life but a Happy Ending":
Margaret Irene (Evers) Jefferson ............................................ 7

CHAPTER 2  "A Place of Sound Discipline":
Kambala Foundation School for Girls ................................ 43

CHAPTER 3  Kambala: Learning to Win, Learning to Lose ................... 62

**Introduction to Part II** ........................................................................ 97

CHAPTER 4  Activism, Education, and Mothers .................................. 101

CHAPTER 5  More Activism:
Challenging Homophobia in Toronto Schools ................ 127

CHAPTER 6  Women's Studies:
Feminists Educating Feminists .......................................... 145

Final Reflections ................................................................................. 163

Endnotes .............................................................................................. 166

Bibliography ....................................................................................... 167

Copyright Acknowledgments ........................................................... 178

Index .................................................................................................... 179

# Acknowledgments

Since this book is largely autobiographical and spans six decades of my life, there are many, many people—family, friends, teachers, colleagues, and students—who have contributed to its creation, perhaps without knowing. To all of you, thank you for what I've learned.

For institutional support, thanks are due to the Department of Sociology and Equity Studies in Education, Ontario Institute for Studies in Education, University of Toronto, my home department since 1996, and to the Department of Adult Education (1991–1995).

Maureen FitzGerald, Liz Green, Nicolas Lenskyj, Kerry Robinson, and an anonymous reviewer provided helpful critical feedback, and Liz did her usual thorough copy-editing. Kambala's archivist, Jenny Bolton, gave me valuable assistance. It was a joy to work again with Althea Prince, managing editor of Women's Press, who offered enthusiastic support throughout the project. Thanks, too, to the production and marketing teams at Women's Press for their important contributions.

Finally, as always, I would like to thank my partner and my children for their love and support.

# Introduction

This is a book of stories about education and women's lives—my mother's and my own. It is biography and autobiography written as social history.

In Part I, I present the background for my mother's narrative, beginning in 1832, when her grandfather arrived in Sydney, Australia, as a convict. The first chapter charts my mother's family history, her childhood and young adult years, and our interconnected lives in the 1940s and 1950s. In the next two chapters, I examine my own girlhood experiences in the 1950s as a child of working-class parents and an outsider in a private girls' school. In this discussion, I reflect on learning lessons about "one's station in life," the influences of female teachers and peers, and my later coming out as a lesbian. Using sources from Australian women's history, women's studies, and critical social theory, I place these two stories in the broader Australian socio-cultural context of 1900–1960.

Part II moves to the Canadian educational context. Chapter 4 documents the interventions of mothers involved in community activism in the 1960s and 1970s in the Toronto Board of Education, and my own experiences in a school-community council. The next chapter examines lesbian and gay activism aimed at educational change in the 1980s and 1990s, including my role on the writing

xi

team that prepared curriculum guidelines on homophobia and sexual orientations for Toronto teachers. Finally, in Chapter 6, I reflect on my experiences as an openly lesbian professor at the Ontario Institute for Studies in Education, University of Toronto, since 1986, and discuss developments in anti-oppression teaching in the university in the 1990s.

# PART I

INTRODUCTION TO PART I

# Sydney, Australia: Two Childhoods

My mother, Margaret Evers, was born in a small country town in western New South Wales (NSW) in 1898, and lived in Sydney from 1902 until her death in 1997. She left school at age 15 and was employed for seven years, mostly in factory work, before marrying in 1921. For most of her adult life, she was occupied with the responsibilities of being a wife and a mother. I was born in Sydney in 1943, and attended Kambala, a private girls' school, until I was 17. I then completed a three-year teaching diploma, taught for two years, married, and moved to Toronto in 1966. I spent most of the next 14 years as a fairly traditional wife and mother until I left the marriage in 1980. Ten years of part-time university studies culminated in a Ph.D. in 1983. I have more than 25 years of teaching experience in Australia and Canada at levels ranging from early childhood to graduate school.

Reflecting on the factors that caused her to imagine her life differently from women of earlier generations, Australian historian Marjorie Theobald (1996: 251) observed that

> for many women of my generation the catalyst was the second women's movement of the 1970s ... My new life as an historian and an academic is lived in the company of another self who

might have lived my mother's life. The legacy of this personal history is clear enough; I am fascinated by the narratives of women's lives interacting with structures of power not of their own making.

While I agree with Theobald's "imaginings," I can also see how my mother might have lived my life had she been born a half century later. Several historical and biographical works inspired this project, including those by Carolyn Steedman (1986), Diane Bell (1987), and Jill Ker Conway (1990, 1994, 2001). Steedman, an English historian, provided an incisive commentary on social mobility when she compared herself, as a woman from a working-class family, to one of her middle-class colleagues: "One hundred years ago," she reflected, "I'd have been cleaning your shoes." In her blend of biography, autobiography, and revisionist feminist history in *Landscape for a Good Woman* (1986), Steedman explored the ways in which girls and women developed class consciousness in postwar England. She found that neither her mother's story nor her own fitted into contemporary historical explanations of the everyday lives of working-class people. Contrary to such accounts, their lives were not marked by emotional or physical sameness, her father was not a strong, constraining force in their lives, and her mother had no overwhelming desire to bear and raise children. Literary portrayals of working-class women were also unhelpful to Steedman in her search, and the purpose of her book was to write working-class women's biography as history.

In the context of Australian women's history, as Patricia Grimshaw (1986) and others have noted, early feminist scholars—Anne Summers (1975) and Miriam Dixson (1976), for example—tended to portray Australian women as victims, "the doormats of the western world," in Dixson's words. Since the mid-1970s, the trend in feminist history has been to "redefine the so-called canons

INTRODUCTION TO PART I

of traditional history so that women's experiences may assume a historical centrality and that women may be recognized as active agents in historical processes" (Grimshaw, 1986: 183–184).

To achieve this goal, historians not only focused on previously neglected dimensions of women's everyday lives, but also examined the gendered nature of relationships between the private realm and the broader social and political context. But this relationship, according to Theobald (1996: 176), is only the starting point for studying "the infinitely more difficult terrain of power, ideologies and subjectivities."

Similarly, Australian sociologist Lesley Johnson (1993: 7) claimed that "feminist history needs to investigate the material and ideological specificities of any particular moment which constitute a group of women as powerless or subordinate." As historians are fond of saying, history begins yesterday, and these guiding principles are relevant to a sociological as well as an historical analysis of women's education in Australia and Canada throughout the 20th century.

A book that investigated the private realm of women, and one that resonated with my own experience, was Diane Bell's *Generations*, an oral and documentary history of 19th- and 20th-century White Australian women. The book was organized around topics that were central to most women's everyday lives: household routines, cooking, the double workday, family traditions, and the "facts of life." To begin with the standpoint of women in the domestic realm, as Bell and her co-researchers did, was to challenge the themes that have long dominated malestream Australian history: Confederation, the World Wars, the Depression, industrial disputes, for example. Women were implicated in all these major events, but the starting point for Bell's participants was the home. As she explained, "The kitchen was a site of political education, of listening to the radio, of analysing the latest strikes while salting pork ..." (Bell, 1987: 260).

Both Bell's and Steedman's work served as a catalyst for me, a fourth-generation Australian woman with rural, working-class, convict roots (through my great-grandfather on my mother's side), to explore the personal histories of women in my extended family. Miriam Dixson (1976: 19) has argued that Australia's colonial and convict history constituted a stigma from which respectable classes in the early settlements had to distance themselves. By the 19th century, she claimed, the problem of the "general Western bourgeois preoccupation with female respectability and domesticity," exacerbated by convictism, had developed into "an extremely defensive version of ultrarespectability and ultradomesticity." In this context, working-class as well as middle-class women experienced pressure to remove themselves from the convict stigma, especially if there was, in fact, a direct link to convict ancestors, as the following account of my mother's family, the Evers, will reveal.

Another influential feminist scholar was Jill Ker Conway, whose three books—*The Road from Coorain* (1990), *True North* (1994), and *A Woman's Education* (2001)—examined her childhood and adolescence in Australia, her academic career in Canada and the United States, and her experiences and reflections as president of Smith College. However, unlike Conway, I am not writing in a purely autobiographical vein, nor do I have any administrative aspirations. My task, as a feminist sociologist, is to interpret my mother's story, my own story, and other historical and contemporary primary sources in light of sociological analyses of women's history and education, community activism, and feminist pedagogy.

Although my approach differs somewhat from Conway's, her description of an autobiographical approach is illuminating:

> The autobiographer writes a narrative where subject and object are intermingled—where knower and the known are part of the

## INTRODUCTION TO PART I

same consciousness. This makes for riveting reading when the narrator can move seamlessly between the selves as object and speaker, providing text which conveys both inner life and external events. (Conway, 1999: vii)

Sue Middleton's 1993 book, *Educating Feminists: Life Histories and Pedagogy*, also served as a model and an inspiration, although I read it after I had written the first draft of this book. Her comments on life history methodology are particularly relevant. Acknowledging that she relied on women's own descriptions and analyses of early experiences in their families and schools, she wrote:

> It was possible for a woman to have been wrong in her interpretation of past events—for example, her mother's expectations, feelings, or motives, or a teacher's prejudices. However, these adult memories and interpretations were accepted as valid because the central concern in the study was not the events themselves but the interpretations the women made of them and the importance the women attached to these interpretations in their becoming feminists and educators. (Middleton, 1993: 68)

Similarly, I acknowledge that my mother's and my stories are largely retrospective adult memories and interpretations. In my own case, like Middleton's participants, I had ample opportunity to revise and reinterpret what I wrote, and the final version, I believe, tells the truth about these specific parts of my life according to my current memory and understanding of events. In the case of my mother's story, she gave me extensive handwritten notes and family history documents in the early 1990s, and I've used several unedited excerpts, with a few explanatory notes, in Chapter 1. My mother knew that I was keenly interested in her early life, both as her daughter and as an historian, and was pleased to know that I presented a conference paper entitled "Mothers, Daughters, Wives: Three Generations of Australian Women" based in part on her life story (Lenskyj, 1991).

My mother's account, as I observe in the next chapter, revealed extensive self-censorship, and I have respected this. However, I have taken responsibility for selectively including my own experiences and memories of family conflict, some of which would probably fall into her "censored" category. In espousing feminists' position that "the personal is political," I am also mindful, thanks to my mentor and friend, Mary O'Brien, that *personal* is not the same as *intimate*, and this distinction has guided my disclosures.

As Middleton explained, she, too, had to decide on the "story" she would tell about herself in her book. She chose to divulge personal details that were sociologically relevant, and omitted parts that she was uncomfortable sharing in a public forum. Like Middleton, I'm not writing in a confessional mode, nor do I necessarily see the telling of my story as therapeutic. I was, and continue to be, a player in the social contexts explored here: Sydney's private schools in the 1950s, Toronto's parent activism in the 1970s, and Toronto's feminist academic community since the 1980s.

# CHAPTER 1

## "... A Bad Start in My Life but a Happy Ending":

### Margaret Irene (Evers) Jefferson

Margaret Evers was born in Molong, a small settlement 172 miles west of Sydney, NSW, on April 20, 1898. A record of events that shaped and changed her life is found in her handwritten account, "The Story of My Life," compiled in July 1982 when she was 84 years old, with a few notes added in the 1990s, and I've used unedited excerpts from her story in this chapter. As I noted earlier, I am interpreting her early experiences using the work of feminist historians such as Diane Bell, Patricia Grimshaw, Carolyn Steedman, Marjorie Theobald, and others.

On the issue of disclosure in women's oral histories, Diane Bell reported:

> The older women recalled their girlhoods in detail most readily, and, although the memories were of hard times, the events were far enough away to be safe to talk about ... The reminiscences did not dwell on alcoholism, although on probing there was plenty of grief ... They were quite explicit about why women stayed in violent marriages or lived at home with parents, but there was also acceptance: "That's how life was; we made the best of it." (Bell, 1987: 47)

Sadly, little has changed for women. "You make your bed, you lie on it" remains the mantra of many unhappy wives, including women of my own generation and my own extended family. Reflecting on her adult life when she was in her 80s and 90s, Margaret Jefferson showed some of the same self-censorship as Bell's respondents, but at times provided illuminating glimpses of her real feelings and reactions to hardship and loss.

The collection of photos and documents that my mother gave me in 1994 when she moved to a nursing home tells much, but not all, of her life story. Having known her for 54 years of my life, with 22 years spent under the same roof, I am able to fill in some of the missing parts from my own experiences and from the stories she told me. I am writing an account that is largely based on these years of shared experiences and conversations, and on the long talks we had on my annual trips to Sydney between 1990 and 1997.

Like many women of her era who assumed kin-keeping responsibilities, Margaret collected more than 70 documents dating from 1891 to 1997, in addition to photograph albums. Margaret's sister, Doris (Evers) McOnie, was another kin-keeper with a particular interest in the Evers' family history, and she gave Margaret several documents, including a notebook entitled "Record of Births, Marriages & Deaths of the Evers' Family, and Other Items of Interest," inscribed "To my sister Maggie from Doris, June 1968." From Doris, Margaret also received a Dickens Birthday Record—a small red leather book with gilt edges—as a 21st birthday present. In it, she entered family and friends' birthdays, and taped newspaper clippings of births, marriages, and deaths, for more than 70 years.

Margaret's collection of treasured items included her 1913 qualifying certificate from the NSW Department of Public Instruction and employers' letters of reference (1916, 1919); newspaper clippings from Molong and Sydney papers (1947–1980s); family passports and birth, marriage, and death certificates; and letters and cards from family and friends (1908–1997). The documents reveal Margaret's fondness for adding marginal notes, usually in ink, apparently with little regard for the "official" status of the original. For example, after decades of answering to the hated name "Maggie" (which in Australian slang connotes someone who chatters too much, like a magpie), she firmly changed it to "Margaret" on her birth certificate and on several other items of identification.

Unfortunately, Margaret's collection dwindled over the years. When she sold the family home in 1978 and moved to a seniors' residence, she either threw out or gave away a lot of family documents. It is illuminating to look at what she *did* keep, especially items that were in her possession for about 80 years before she passed them on to me. It seems that she retained the most salient documents, those that reminded her of very happy or very sad times: a postcard from her mother dated 1908, pencil drawings that she had completed as a teenager, the receipt for baby Joan's funeral, her son Bill's note when he left home, and the ticket from her 1982 cruise to Fiji. One of the most poignant items is an unsigned Golden Wedding Anniversary greeting card, a sad reminder of her lonely celebration on July 2, 1971. Her husband Bill, aged 90 and in failing health and low spirits by this time, had shown no interest in the anniversary, so Margaret bought the card for herself, added it to her collection of treasures, and celebrated the event by buying a jug of beer to share with her friends at the women's bowling club.

The items that Margaret saved over the years give the impression that she was actively selecting what should go into her personal time capsule. Looking at my own smaller collection from the first 35 or so years of my life—that is, before my training in history and sociology—I realize that I used to follow similar selection criteria and would keep only a few samples from various periods. Now, I consider the potential historical interest before throwing out anything.

## The Evers Family

Starting with the Evers' family history, I'll sketch the social and historical context into which Margaret was born. Fortunately, much of the background has been recorded in an unpublished booklet, *A Brief History of the Evers' Family*, that was compiled by a distant relative, Daphne Riley, in 1967, and Margaret's sister, Doris, made a handwritten copy for her the same year.

In 1836, Jane Johnson, my great-grandmother on my mother's side, was born in the military barracks on George Street, Sydney. Her father, Samuel, was the pay sergeant for the 17th Middlesex Regiment, which had escorted convicts from England. At this stage, European settlement in Australia had only a 60-year history. Sydney was established as a penal colony in 1787, and convicts from England and Ireland were transported there until the 1850s. Nearly all were from the labouring classes, and about 80 percent had been convicted of larceny of various kinds (Robson, 1994). As late as 1828, 46 percent of the NSW population were convicts, with 16,442 males and only 2,577 females (Summers, 1975: 275).

The Johnson family moved to central NSW when Jane was about 11. She was subsequently employed by John Smith, a Member of the NSW Legislative Assembly, as a "nurse girl" for the Smith children at Gamboola, a sheep and cattle station. At this time, the only buildings where the town of Molong now stands were the Gamboola homestead and two other houses (Riley, 1967).

Jane became the first bush nurse and midwife in the area. Her work, as well as her father's military employment, would have served, to some extent, to distance the Johnson family from the colonial convict stigma. Yet, both Jane and her sister Eliza subsequently married men who had come to Australia as convicts.

My aunt's brief handwritten notes on the family history, dated 1968, reflect the secrecy surrounding convict ancestors at that time.

# "... A BAD START IN MY LIFE BUT A HAPPY ENDING"

On the topic of my great-grandfather's roots, she added the cryptic note "(details unknown) we never saw or heard anything of his life." Daphne Riley (1967) was more circumspect (and it appears that her account has incorrect dates):

> Naturally, as will happen in a country so vast, and yet so young, a great deal of the early life of one of the first settlers in Molong, namely Titus Evers, is lost. We do know that he was born in Yorkshire, England, in 1813, and arrived in Australia at the age of 36, son of Robert Evers.

Ironically, as Australian historians subsequently discovered, it was often easier to find information on ancestors who were convicts than on those who were not.

In the same vein, the 1956 *Molong Express* obituary of Mrs. Mary Kerr Evers, my maternal grandmother, stated that her late husband, Samuel, had been the "son of the oldest pioneering family of the town," but it made no reference to his father's convict roots—a typical omission in that era. As a journalist observed in 1947, most Australians felt "that the possession of a convict as an ancestor may be damaging to their own reputation" (cited in Reakes, 1987).

The Evers' "family secret" was publicly disclosed in a *Molong Express* story in 1989, at a time when convict roots were not only acceptable, but even fashionable. By the 1980s, some Australians were disappointed when they did *not* find a convict ancestor, according to Janet Reakes, whose book *How to Trace Your Convict Ancestors* was published by a mainstream Australian publisher, Hale & Iremonger, in 1987.

According to the 1989 account, Titus Evers, my great-grandfather, was born in Yorkshire in 1811. In 1832, he was charged with illegally entering the house of a Joseph Sanderson. He pleaded guilty and was sentenced to death, but the sentence was commuted to 14 years' servitude in NSW. He arrived in Sydney on the *Parmelia* on November 16, 1832. A cloth weaver by trade, he was assigned to William Charles Wentworth, later known for his exploration of the Blue Mountains (*Molong Express*, 1989).

Titus began serving his sentence in the Bathurst district of central NSW, and was granted a ticket-of-leave (pardon) after seven years. He was now free to take employment or to become self-employed, and to acquire property, as long as he resided within the Bathurst district and attended church every week. Years later, he worked near Orange, where he met Jane Johnson, and they were married on January 25, 1852.

In 1853, Titus, Jane, and their infant son, William, moved to Molong. They had seven sons and five daughters, two of whom died in early childhood. William narrowly escaped drowning, at four weeks of age, when Jane was taking him on horseback from the settlement of Blackman's Swamp, his birthplace, to Molong, a distance of about 15 miles. As Doris described it, Jane "had a terrifying experience at Broken Shaft Creek a few miles out when the baby was dropped into the water as the horse rushed to the creek for a drink. She rescued him and went on her way." (William went on to live to the age of 93.)

## Life on the Land

Titus worked as a shepherd on Smith's property and soon earned a reputation for his ability to count up to 9,000 head of sheep. Working alone or in pairs for months at a stretch, a shepherd led a lonely life, sleeping in a rough shelter called a shepherd's watch box with dogs as company.

Keeping cattle contained in one area presented a different challenge, and in about 1861 John Smith came up with the idea of

## "... A BAD START IN MY LIFE BUT A HAPPY ENDING"

engaging Titus and two other men to enclose a 90-acre paddock. Instead of the usual brush or post-and-rail, the new fence was to be constructed of five strands of heavy wire stretched between wooden posts. Heralded as the first "wire paddock" west of the Great Dividing Range, its history was celebrated in 1989 when a sign was erected on the site. An article in the *Molong Express* noted approvingly that it was "the forerunner of hundreds of thousands of miles of 'wire fences' since erected through western NSW"—in that author's view, a mark of progress (*Molong Express*, 1989).

From the Aboriginal perspective, however, fences symbolized dispossession. They had already suffered decades of colonial oppression, ranging from massacres to desecration of their sacred land, and the fence represented "the ultimate statement of European settlement." As historian and author Tom Keneally convincingly argued:

> Far more than the spreading of disease, or the poisoning of flour issued to tribespeople, or the hunting of Aboriginals as if they were game ... the fence interrupted the access of tribes to the Dreaming [sacred ancestral] trails and so helped wither the Aboriginal soul. (Keneally, 1987: 41)

European concepts of property ownership included marking boundaries, planting crops, and building permanent shelters, whereas tribal Aboriginals followed the trails between waterholes, hunting, fishing, and digging for food. For more than two centuries, Europeans' claim that no one had owned the land before the arrival of the First Fleet from England in 1788—the concept of *terra nullius*—was used to justify the dispossession of Indigenous people. It was not until the 1990s that Native Title Acts took a broader view: unless title had been extinguished under an Act of government, Aboriginals could claim land if they provided geographic and genealogical evidence of ongoing observance of traditional laws and customs.

## The Evers' Sons

Three of the Evers' sons, William, Edwin, and Samuel, also worked as shepherds in their adolescent years. As adults, William and Edwin bought land in Molong and nearby districts; William subsequently became a Molong alderman and an Amaroo Shire councillor, and both he and his wife Sophia were widely recognized in the community for their charitable work.

Samuel's adult life took a different turn. Born in Molong on June 17, 1862, my grandfather had an unhappy boyhood and adolescence working as a shepherd under his father's supervision. Although he never attended school, he taught himself to read and write, and composed poetry during the long nights in the bush. Years later, one of his poems, "Our Lonely Camp at Night," written "near Dandaloo, Bogan River," was published in a Molong newspaper (1892), and Doris included it in her handwritten Evers' family record.

According to Daphne Riley's account of Sam's adolescence, "the loneliness and monotony of the job was so distressing to this bright boy that, when his pleadings to be released were ignored, he left without any training, and became one of the first bush carpenters" (Riley, 1967). His years as a shepherd may have been a factor in his drinking problem. As W.R. Glasson explained in his history of Australian shepherds, these men often lived for the day, only about three times per year, when they could return to the station homestead to pick up their paycheques.

> On reaching town ... he would first buy some badly needed clothes and then, typical of so many of his day, he would place

the balance of his money on the hotel bar and ask to be told when it was "cut out." (Glasson, 1941: n.p.)

Sam's poem, cited earlier, included somewhat apologetic lines about getting drunk: "We don't mean to get 'tight'/but make straight home to our wives and friends/far from our lonely camp at night."

## The McCallums Come to Molong

Mary Kerr McCallum, my grandmother, was the daughter of Sarah (McLean) and Duncan McCallum; she was born in Holytown, Lanarkshire, Scotland, on April 14, 1868. In a letter written to my mother in the 1940s, Mary explained, "My father died when I was between 4 and 6 years so soon after we went to live with our Grandma at Muirkirk-Ayrshire. Grandma was a widow so company for all of us. Aunty [Maggie] would have been very young then. We lived at Muirkirk until we came out here [to Australia]." Her father was killed when he was thrown from a buggy. On February 2, 1889, the McCallum family—mother and two adult daughters—sailed from Tilbury Docks, London, for Sydney.

Mary's uncle, Dr. Andrew Ross (1829–1910), had travelled to Sydney more than 30 years earlier, in 1857, as the medical officer on an immigration ship. He settled in Molong and became a prominent public figure: first medical officer, registrar, coroner, and public vaccinator in the district; Member of the Legislative Assembly for 24 years; founder of the *Molong Argus* newspaper in 1893; and contributor of articles to the *NSW Medical Gazette* (University of Melbourne, 2003).

According to Doris's notes, Dr. Ross welcomed his sister and nieces when they arrived in Sydney, and Mary lived with him and his wife in Molong before her marriage. However, despite his privileged position, it does not appear that he continued to help Mary during the financially and emotionally troubled years of her marriage.

Mary was a qualified schoolteacher, and the schoolhouse where she taught was a small hut of wattle-and-daub (a weave of green timber with the gaps plugged with mud) at Peabody, the property owned many decades later by one of the more successful Evers brothers, William. It appears that Sam and Mary met soon after she arrived in the Molong district, and they married in October 1891. Over the next 18 years, Mary had 10 children—seven sons and three daughters. My mother, Margaret, was their fifth child and youngest daughter, born on April 20, 1898.

In my mother's collection was a small but significant piece of paper: a corner torn from a letter, which had the address, "Peabody, Molong" and the date "10th October, 1891" in Mary's writing. My mother had added the words "my mother's wedding date" and "7th [October]." Since Mary and Sam's first child, Eddie, was born on November 20, 1891—that is, about six weeks after the wedding—this might explain the fact that my mother kept this piece of paper for so long. Not only would a "heavily pregnant" unmarried teacher have attracted the attention of the rural landowning class and the residing medical officer (her uncle), but one can imagine how Mary's dour Presbyterian mother might have received the news.

As late as the 1980s, the fact that one of my elderly relatives had been pregnant when she got married in 1915 was still treated as a (widely known) "family secret." The discourse of sexuality—phrases like "shotgun wedding," "living in sin," "in the family way," and "illegitimate child" (this phrase from my mother's notes on the Evers' family tree)—reflected a Victorian view of sexuality that continued to shape the attitudes of older Australians well into the 20th century. The "sexual revolution" of the 1960s had minimal impact on my mother's world view or on her language. "Pregnant" was a word she avoided ("expecting" was her preferred term), menopause was "change of life," and menstruation, inexplicably, went by the code word "James."

## Growing Up "in the Bush"

Both Margaret and her older sister Doris had lasting memories of poverty and hardship as young children growing up in Molong. This is a short account that Doris wrote in 1972 when she was almost 80 years old:

> My mother cooked stinging nettles and my father used to gather horehound that grew in a paddock next to our old home in Boree Hollow. He made horehound beer. Shepherds would also boil the nettles, known as "shepherd's cabbage," and eat them with their dry corned beef and damper [homemade bread]. Many a time too I had to go with him through the bush and gather opossums he had snared to sell the skins, also trapped rabbits ...
>
> The children of today have no conception of what we had to do in our day and the hardship we endured, floods, getting out of the house in the middle of the night, had to go to a neighbour's on the hill and dear Mum would have to make a damper at their place with some flour given to us by neighbour and baked in open fire place in ashes as shepherds did. On returning home when the weather subsided—our fowls were washed away, also our toilet, a wooden structure, and old [sewage] pans would be gone. I have written a book on my life so as the years go by the next generation in the family will know what we kids went through, me being the eldest "copped the lot."

Unfortunately, it appears that the book to which Doris referred was not located after her death.

Margaret also had vivid and lasting memories of the flood:

> I remember the flood at Molong when I was about 3 years old. We lived next to a creek where we watched so many sheep and poultry being washed away. We had a four poster bed and everything possible was thrown up onto the cover. We were inside when my Dad opened the back door, then the water came pouring into the house. Our Dad started carrying us up the hill to relations. A week later, we returned to the clearing up.

## Life with Grandma McCallum

When Margaret was about five, her mother sent her to Sydney to live with Grandma McCallum because she could not afford to keep so many children at home. Her grandmother needed help operating her boarding house, and Margaret, as the youngest girl in the family, could be spared, while the two older girls could not. In Margaret's account, she left Molong thinking the Sydney trip was merely a holiday.

> The next memory was the night I left Molong with my Cousin Louie Ross, she was going to Sydney and my dear Mother sent me down with her to visit her Mother and Sister, my Grandmother and Aunty Maggie. I can still see my dear Mum standing with some of our family when the train pulled out. My luggage consisted of an Arnott's Biscuit tin ... At last we arrived at 229 Barcom Avenue Darlinghurst that was to be my home until I left about 15 years later.

In the late 1800s and early decades of the 20th century, as historian David Harris explained, the inner-suburban rental market in

## "... A BAD START IN MY LIFE BUT A HAPPY ENDING"

cities such as Sydney and Melbourne comprised mostly tenements, flats, and boarding houses, the latter usually operated by women. In 1901, for example, one in ten working women in the state of Victoria ran a boarding house (Harris, 1988: 48). Those who rented these accommodations were mostly single employed men and women. Labour historian Edna Ryan identified the women who took in boarders, did laundry or sewing at home, or went out to do domestic and child-care work as "invisible breadwinners" (Ryan, 1986: 267; see also Bryson, 1994).

Many women, such as Sarah McCallum, were widows supporting themselves and their families, and their role in the informal economy was often overlooked in official census figures. My mother's account shows how she herself made significant contributions to the informal economy, despite her young age.

> I had rather a hard life with my Grandma. She also had boarders besides doing sewing at home for Farmers [department store] where my Aunty [Maggie] worked in their workroom. I had to clean the fuel stove and polish it with black stuff. We had a brick yard and I had to get down on my knees and scrub ...
>
> My Grandma made me do the washing up and I was supposed to use the water in the copper [metal boiler for laundry] when hot after everyone had their clothes washed in it. I seemed to know this was wrong and I would boil a kettle on the stove and use it. If I got caught a smack across the face I would get, if I did not have an apron, another smack across the face ...
>
> If a fly went into the boarder's cup of tea we just took it out and served the tea ...
>
> I did have a hard time living at 229. Every Saturday I would be sent down to Roslyn Street to a Miss Foley who was my aunty's boss at work and I would have so many rooms to clean upstairs and downstairs. By the time I got to kitchen pantry and laundry I was

beginning to get a little tired, however I would receive a 1/- [one shilling] or sixpence, also I got pieces of material for skirts, etc. ...

Grandma would reply to advertisements in the Herald for someone wanting board and I would have to take letters into town to the Herald office in Hunter Street ...

We had friends near Coogee Beach, I would take them stale bread for their fowls, they also had an orchard, in exchange I would bring home fruit vegetables and eggs.

## Learning Her Place

This life would have been difficult for any child, but for Margaret there were added hardships. Living away from her parents and siblings, she was under the control of a strict Scottish Presbyterian grandmother who seemed to hold what Edna Ryan (1986: 267) described as "a relic of the slave-driving psychology ... concerning female workers." Overall, Margaret seems to have been treated as a domestic slave, and there were times when she literally lived "below stairs."

> My grandmother often has country visitors and we would have to sleep in the kitchen. If there was someone else there we would have to sleep under the stairs (it was a 2 storey house) which was so very dark and no ventilation. Grandma and I used to sleep on a little three quarter bed in the back room above the stove.

Her grandmother's approach to child rearing can only be described as brutal. In Margaret's words:

> My memory goes back to my younger days, if I had done something wrong, and my Grandmother would send me upstairs, and tell me to take all my clothes off, and up she would come

> with a strap, what was called a cat and nine tails, I wonder why those strap marks ever disappeared.

This is puzzling as well as disturbing. Why would an elderly Scottish woman use as an implement of punishment a cat-o'-nine-tails, which was a rope whip with nine knotted lashes generally reserved for disciplining prisoners and military men? Perhaps the answer lies in a combination of Scottish and Australian disciplinary practices, both of which were notoriously nasty. As late as the 1930s, under the Scottish legal system, it was common for judges to order the "birching" of juvenile male offenders, who were flogged on the bare buttocks with a birch rod, a bundle of twigs resembling a gardener's broom (Mahood, 2002). And in Queensland, Australia, there were examples of floggings using the cat-o'-nine-tails as late as World War II, the victims being Aboriginal children in the Catholic mission school system (God's Enforcers, 2003). Priests and nuns, as well as other church-affiliated "missionaries," were infamous for their sadistic, racist treatment of Aboriginal children who had been forcibly removed from their families of origin; the 2002 film *Rabbitproof Fence* documented these abuses in graphic detail.

There is a chance, I would like to believe, that Margaret may have been referring to a leather strap of the kind used in Australian schools until the 1980s. (It was not until 1983 that the first Australian state, Victoria, abolished strapping in schools; in contrast, the Toronto Board of Education prohibited corporal punishment in 1971.) Regardless of the actual implement, the kind of punishment administered by Sarah McCallum was unusually brutal even for that era, and Margaret longed to go home.

> I used to get so very homesick then I would pack my biscuit tin and tie it up with string, and off I would go up the hill to Oxford

St. only short distance to the Hotel at corner which kept open till 10 pm. Sometimes I would get as far as Taylor's Square and the string would break and home I would come again.

## Apprenticeship in Domesticity

Margaret received early training—again, not always pleasant—in thrifty household management.

> My Grandmother would send me back to the grocers with bad eggs, she would put them in a bucket of water and they would just float. How I hated taking them back, but I generally got them replaced ...
> Things were so very cheap, I would go to the fruit shop on Saturday and get a shilling's worth of mixed fruit for the boarders' Sunday dinner and there was nearly enough to last for the week. The rabbit man would go around in his cart selling rabbits and would skin them while I waited, always followed by lots of dogs waiting for bits and pieces .... then we also got pigeons and I had to clean and pluck them and they made lovely pies, the meat was darker than fowl. Grandma always killed the fowl by cutting off its head with a knife. I was given the job to kill one, so on to the block it went and I would attempt to cut off its head. I would only have been about 12.

Curiously, while her grandmother seemed to have devoted time and effort to Margaret's training as a domestic helper, she neglected other areas.

> My grandma never taught me to wash my hands and face, my Mother came to see us and she asked me if I washed in the morn-

ing and night and I said no so it was her that helped me keep clean, no toothbrushes ... The weekend was the time everyone had a bath only once a week ... only changed our clothes once a week.

A postcard to "Miss M. Evers" from her mother, dated October 16, 1908, is the oldest piece of correspondence in Margaret's collection. Printed in Germany, it had an embossed illustration of pansies and "Remembrance from Mother" outlined in glitter. In view of later revelations about her childhood, it is likely that her mother's message evoked mixed feelings in the 10-year-old Margaret: "... I hope you and G. Ma are in your usual health. (I hope) Be a good girl & *do what you can to help her*" (emphasis added).

## School Days, Happy Days

Fortunately for Margaret, elementary education had become compulsory in NSW for children aged six to fourteen as a result of the 1880 Public Instruction Act, which provided "free" education until high school. The attendance law was not stringently enforced, and in the period 1880–1920 female attendance represented only about 60–70 percent of their actual enrolment, largely as a result of girls being kept home to help their mothers with housework and child care. There was a significant gender gap, too, in public school enrolment; in 1900, boys' enrolment outnumbered girls' by 10,000 (Kyle, 1986: 44–45, 228).

School offered Margaret some much-needed respite from domestic chores and her grandmother's wrath, and her attendance record was excellent. In December 1906, at the end of upper second class, she received a prize for "attendance and quarterly exams": a book entitled *The Children's Own Magazine*, which comprised a collection of stories, poems, puzzles, and "Sunday evening talks" full of uplifting religious messages.

> When I was five I want to Albion St. Public school, I did enjoy going to school. (P.S. Years after, my son went to the same school but it was a Technical College then.) I never missed one day from school, rain or shine I got there.
>
> Every Empire Day 24th May our classes would march to the Victoria Barracks and listen to speeches and sing patriotic songs like Advance Australia Fair ...
>
> Every Thursday when I was old enough, our class went to Paddington Public School for cookery lessons. Thursdays would not come around quick enough for me. I got a silver medal which I have given to my Granddaughter Lisa.

By 1890, every girl in fifth class had to take a weekly cookery class for three months, and cookery and domestic science became the alternative subject to natural science for girls in NSW public schools. And by the early 1900s, the interventions of middle-class reformers such as the National Council of Women, which called for mandatory domestic science for high school girls of "the [social] class that needs it the most ... poorer people," had borne fruit. Mathematics, French, and Latin were now viewed as less important than the subjects that would prepare girls for matrimony, a state widely seen as "the ultimate goal of nearly every girl" (Kyle, 1986: 55).

Apart from the predictable rhetoric about preparing the next generation of wives and mothers to build a healthier and more moral society, the "servant problem" was a high priority for the middle-class proponents of domestic science, who wanted trained, malleable girls to clean their houses. Increasingly, working-class girls were opting for commercial and industrial employment, which offered better working conditions, although in 1901 almost half of employed women were still in domestic service (Kyle, 1986; Markey, 1980: 87).

Although girls such as Margaret would have been the targets of these reformers' efforts, she had an advantage as a student of

# "... A BAD START IN MY LIFE BUT A HAPPY ENDING"

Albion Street Superior Public School. This category of "superior public schools," first established in NSW in the 1880s, offered higher primary classes in local public schools—an attractive option for working-class students, especially girls, whose parents were unwilling or unable to pay the fees that public high schools charged at that time. Despite the gender-specific subjects listed on the official curriculum, some girls in superior public schools in this era successfully completed examinations in subjects such as French, German, algebra, geometry, and geology (Kyle, 1986: 110). Margaret studied academic as well as domestic subjects, and kept her German textbook, *German without Tears*, for more than 50 years as a souvenir of her school days.

Unlike the women in Diane Bell's study (1987: Chapter 10), who attributed a lifelong love of books to their positive childhood experiences, Margaret seemed to have little interest in reading. No doubt her mother and grandmother would have lacked the discretionary income to purchase books, and the school prize mentioned earlier was the only book in her collection. I recall my parents' traditional reading patterns when I was young: my father read the *Sydney Morning Herald* and borrowed westerns (Zane Grey's, in particular) from the library, while my mother read the *Women's Weekly* and the occasional romantic novel. Apart from my brother's and my own collections, there were very few books in our house. Ones I recall are the animal novel *Man-Shy* by Frank Dalby Davison, who was a family friend, a Webster's dictionary, the ubiquitous *Pears' Cyclopaedia* (courtesy of the Pears' soap people), one other encyclopedia, a Bible, and a home remedies book that my mother kept in her bedside cabinet. Again, my parents' working-class origins probably account for the low priority placed on purchasing books when they could easily be borrowed from the library.

A LOT TO LEARN

## Safe at Home?

Reflecting on Sydney in the first decade of the 20th century, Margaret stated: "Everyone was safe in those days on the street, no assaults or robbery ... How the years have changed, even children were safe going everywhere." In reality, women and children were not necessarily "safe" outside or inside the home, as her own experiences demonstrate.

Margaret went back to Molong to see her family during school holidays, and her memories of this period shed light on Mary Evers's life: an educated woman, now in her 40s, with nine children at home, living in poverty with an abusive husband who had a drinking problem.

> When I was older, I would go home to Molong for my school holidays, I can still see my Grandma putting me through the train window to get a seat, then the guard would open door and look at tickets. I would be put in the care of a passenger and my family would meet me at Molong.
>
> It was really lovely when I went home for school holidays except when my Father was drunk, and then Oh Boy it was really terrible. My dear Mother would have to hide for days and the family would take her meals. At times the family would take out court orders to stop him buying drink but always some of his mates would sell it to him for a price.

The passing reference to her mother's hiding is almost certainly an indication that Sam was physically abusive toward her when he was drunk.

> One time my mother came to Sydney I must have been about 14, I went home to look after my brothers who were at school, we

# "... A BAD START IN MY LIFE BUT A HAPPY ENDING"

had nothing to eat but pumpkins, in pies, mashed or just plain. Dad killed a pig but no we got no pig. How we all longed for a lovely meal of pork.

It was really frightening waiting for my Dad to come home and oh boy, the language. Some nights he would take a short cut home through the rock path and would fall and lie there wet or fine. He was what one would call a born drunkard.

We had several homes, the last but one was just a tumbled old place, no stove, no nothing. Until my dear eldest brother pulled down the old place, and with the help of the family built a lovely comfortable home. Dear Eddie, he passed away not too many years after.

Eddie died at age 43 (from pneumonia), in contrast to the mostly long-lived Evers siblings, including Doris, 103; Evelyn (Tottie), 100; Margaret, 99; and Stan, 97. Their parents, Mary and Sam, lived to 88 and 84 respectively. For a family of children born in Molong in the late 1800s, the longevity of those who survived infancy was noteworthy. With the infant mortality in Australia peaking in the 1870s and 1880s, there were several infant deaths in the Evers family. Australia's maternal mortality rates, too, exceeded those of many European countries well into the 1930s (Matthews, 1984: 32–33).

A *Life Events Index* (2003), based on 1880s editions of the *Molong Express*, indicated numerous deaths among children and adolescents, with causes ranging from accidental drowning, choking, and scalding, to diseases such as bronchitis, diphtheria, and fever. Margaret considered two childhood accidents worthy of inclusion in her memoirs: one sustained as a four-year-old when she cut her hand on an axe, leaving her with a deformed finger, and another when she cut her foot while walking through the creek.

I remember my grandmother's new house from two visits to

Molong with my mother when I was three and ten. It had a central hallway, a veranda on three sides, and a "sleep-out" with louvred windows—all features typical of country houses, but fascinating for a city child. There was a cold water tap in the kitchen over a drain in the floor, but no kitchen sink, just an enamel basin for washing dishes. Large kettles of water were kept hot on the wood-burning kitchen stove. Every couple of days, I had a bath in a big tub in front of the living room fire. The indoor bathroom was rarely used since the hot water heater needed wood chips for fuel and was therefore too labour-intensive for my grandmother. The toilet (dunny) was in the backyard and the "sewage man" came in his truck to collect the pans once a week. Living alone in her 80s, my grandmother kept chickens for eggs and for an occasional chicken dinner. Two sons who lived in Molong—one in the house next door—helped with shopping, chopping wood, and other heavy work around the house and yard.

## A Working Woman, 1913–1921

Margaret's first job was in a printing office, where she was paid 10 shillings per week; 5 shillings went to her grandmother for room and board. Among the documents that she kept were reference letters from two former employers: Ford & Kent, "Manufacturers of costumes [suits], blouses, skirts, children's garments, Etc," dated May 22, 1916, and Anthony Hordern and Sons, Universal Providers, dated March 16, 1919. It seems that she changed jobs frequently of her own accord. Her second job, as presser and folder at Ford & Kent, lasted 18 months and paid 30 shillings a week—a significant increase over her first pay—and this employer considered her to be "a conscientious and energetic worker." She held the Hordern's job as presser in an embroidery factory for only eight months, but was described as "good" in terms of personal character, business ability, and attendance. Then, for a short period, she worked as a mother's helper. Her occupation in 1921, at a weekly wage of 55 shillings, was as an embroidery inspector at the Belfast Linen factory, which produced household linens. Some of their products—tablecloths and pillowcases—were still in use in our home in the 1940s.

Female employees earned significantly less than males, and with trade unions advocating a male family wage in the early 1900s, there was no incentive for employers to raise female wages. Records of comparable weekly wages in 1905 and 1906 included: a female office cleaner, 12 shillings; a male labourer or carter, 42 shillings; a male shop assistant (viewed as a feminized occupation), 30–40 shillings (Ryan, 1986: 265, 267).

## A Married Woman

My mother's marriage, at age 23, provided some financial security and a route to social mobility, although she would probably have valued the first more highly than the second. My father, Bill Jefferson, was a well-established businessman who had emigrated from northern England. His father and some of his brothers were fishermen, but he had completed his apprenticeship as a builder and carpenter, and in about 1911 left England with his brother, Charlie, to set up their own successful building company in Vancouver, Canada. He was 39 years old when they married, but the reasons for his relatively late marriage are not known.

In 1918, Bill came to Australia and boarded with my great-grandmother, who was still operating the boarding house even when she was in her 70s. Here is my mother's account:

# A LOT TO LEARN

> In 1918 I lived with my grandmother in Oatley Road, Paddington. Grandma kept boarders, Bill came to board here. Well as time went on we became very friendly and went to the pictures, etc. At this time Bill was not building, but was in partnership with two other mates, running a business in Bathurst St. Sydney called the Dandy Manufacturing Company, they made mops and other household goods from sheepskins. In April 1919 Bill went to America and Canada. It was very sad for me, I felt so lonely. He had to go there to settle his business with his building partners, which proved very successful.

Margaret and Bill planned a wedding for July 2, 1921, at 7.30 p.m., after which they were to move into a house at Spencer Street, Rose Bay, that Bill had bought. It appears that there was some secrecy surrounding the wedding plans. Like many women, Margaret remembered the precise details of the day all her life.

> I was 23 and Bill 2 months off 40. I moved from the Girls' Friendly Society on the Friday and took delivery of the furniture we bought and stayed the night there, then Bill came out on the Saturday and we got the tram into town and I remember so well, we went into Sargents and had meat pies for tea and then walked to St. Stephens Church in Phillip Street to be married ... what a shock I got when I walked down the aisle to see my sister and Grandma sitting there ... my sister [looking] as much as to say we tricked you ...

Their first daughter, Joan, born at Nurse Barber's maternity home at Rose Bay on October 10, 1924, died after one day. As Margaret wrote years later, "I thought I would never get over it." She kept several records of the sad event: the baby's birth certificate, receipts from Carter's Funerals and South Head Cemetery, and a

# "... A BAD START IN MY LIFE BUT A HAPPY ENDING"

clipping of the *Sydney Morning Herald* birth announcement. In 1925, Bill and Margaret made a fresh start by moving to Vaucluse to live in one of the semi-detached houses that Bill had recently built.

Seven years passed before Margaret became pregnant again. Like other married women of that era, she spent much of her time doing housework: shopping, cooking, cleaning, knitting, sewing, mending clothes, baking, and jam making. Taking pride in a clean and attractive home—a two-bedroom house that must have seemed luxurious compared to her grandmother's and mother's residences—she made curtains, tablecloths, and bedcovers on the treadle sewing machine. Decades later, on the same sewing machine, my 71-year-old mother hemmed crib sheets when her two youngest grandchildren (my children) had their first holiday in Sydney.

Throughout the 1930s, Margaret and Bill had several friends in the now middle-class eastern suburbs, and were part of a group that played cards and socialized on weekends. Unlike most Australians, Margaret disliked swimming and the beach—probably the aftermath of a childhood experience when she almost drowned in a crowded public swimming pool. After her early years with her grandmother and her later paid employment, these years offered more leisure than she had ever had, but, with the ups and downs of marriage to a man with a volatile temper, they were not particularly happy ones.

On April 29, 1930, Margaret and Bill sailed for Canada and the United States on the *Niagara*, the first time that Margaret had travelled more than about 200 miles from home. Her mother came to Sydney to join the friends who wished them bon voyage, and on August 8, 1930, she wrote:

> You looked so lovely we all thought with all your excitement etc. you were just your old self. The costume [suit], pink front & hat etc. suited you good ... all went well and I was glad I was amongst

31

the great number of friends to see you sail. You are quite a happy family these days & I hope all have a pleasant time together.

The not-so-veiled allusions to the difficult years of marriage after baby Joan's death suggest that Margaret confided in her mother, and no doubt gained support from her, mostly through letters. It is significant, too, that, of the large number of letters that Margaret received from her mother over a 40-year period, she saved this one.

Another letter in her collection was written by her father on June 19, 1934. "Just a few lines to let you know that I'm still in the land of the living ... I hope you will excuse bad writing for writing is not my game." Despite his self-taught reading and writing skills, and his disclaimer, the letter is well written and lovingly expressed, ending "with fondest love and kisses from your affectionate father, Sam."

The overseas trip, which included stops at Vancouver, Banff, Seattle, Los Angeles, San Francisco, Suva, and Honolulu, opened Margaret's eyes to the excitement of travel, and she always encouraged me to "see the world." Her dream of going on a second boat cruise was not realized for more than 50 years when, at the age of 84, she and a friend sailed to Fiji on the *Oriana*.

Their son, Bill (Billie), was born in July 1931, this time at home with a private nurse as well as a doctor in attendance as an added safety precaution. "How overjoyed we were," Margaret wrote in her memoirs. Bill attended Vaucluse Public School, and Margaret was involved in the school's Parents' and Citizens' Association. He later went to Sydney Boys' Technical High School, in the same building that used to house Margaret's public school.

In 1940, Margaret was one of the founding members of the Vaucluse Ladies' Bowling Club (lawn bowls), and was the proud winner of the club's first singles championship. She continued playing for more than three decades and then had the honour of

# "... A BAD START IN MY LIFE BUT A HAPPY ENDING"

serving as the club's patron until 1977. In many respects, her life was typical of a middle-class wife and mother of that era, although her roots were firmly in the working class.

My mother was almost 45 and my father 61 when I was born in 1943. She would sometimes mention that I was an "afterthought" and would hint that if I hadn't been born, she might have considered leaving my father. I didn't take that to mean that she had regrets, since she always gave me her unqualified love. In her written memoirs, she confined herself to understatements: "We had a great many ups and downs during our married life." Remembering the 1940s, as a mother of an adolescent son and a baby, she wrote, "They were happy days. We did have our bad times but all's well that ends well."

The women in Diane Bell's study, "dutiful wives and daughters to the end," showed similar reluctance to allow negative assessments of abusive or alcoholic husbands or fathers to be published. For over 20 years, I witnessed my father's anger over seemingly insignificant things, invariably at dinnertime, and his subsequent silent treatment of my mother, sometimes lasting up to two weeks. There was no doubt who was "boss" in our family. As a child, I assumed the man ruled in every family and was amazed to hear one of my mother's friends telling her that she was in charge; I think my mother shared my surprise.

Margaret's generally optimistic spirit helped to carry her through the hard times at home. One of the many songs she would sing while doing the housework was "Look for the silver lining / whene'er a dark cloud appears on the blue ..." Hosing the garden or going for a walk around the block were among the other coping strategies she used to avoid my father's bad temper. Not a religious or church-going person, she nevertheless said her prayers regularly—probably every night of her life—and taught me to do the same.

A LOT TO LEARN

## My Mother, My Father, Myself

In her memoir, Margaret claimed—mistakenly, I believe—that she was not "clever enough" to stay in school, and left when she was 15. Since it was uncharacteristic of her to imply a low sense of self-worth, it seems likely that she wanted the economic independence that paid employment offered. She had wanted to be a schoolteacher, and in a sense became one when she had children of her own. She took great pleasure in teaching me skills ranging from reading and writing to cooking and cleaning. Happily, she did not follow her grandmother's coercive approach, a typical example of which she recalled in her memoirs: "I learned to mend socks at an early age, I would say good night and then [I was] stopped [by Grandma] and brought back to learn to darn socks."

Under my mother's watchful eye at the kitchen table, suitably protected with newspaper, I learned how to write with a pen and ink—dipping the pen carefully in the bottle of blue Quink Ink, wiping off surplus drips, using blotting paper—long before we were taught this skill at school. Having practised successfully on scrap paper, I was then allowed to write a real letter in ink to my grandmother, which, began, as usual, "Dear G. Ma, how are you?" Watching my mother cooking, cleaning, gardening, dressmaking, and mending, I exemplified the child who learned "at her mother's knee." From a contemporary perspective, these lessons might seem oppressively *feminine*, but, to me, they were treasured opportunities to feel a sense of achievement.

Despite his many traditional attitudes, my father was also happy to have me watch him in his workshop and to teach me some carpentry skills. He gave me my own small hammer, wood, and nails, with which I usually constructed boats. Throughout the many years that my mother was in poor health, he washed the breakfast dishes and swept the kitchen floor every morning, as well as taking me on weekend outings. He usually complied with my requests to go swimming in summer and to feed the ducks in Centennial Park in winter. Even going "for a run to the pub" was considered "an outing," especially if his destination was the Astra Hotel at Bondi Beach. He would park on Campbell Parade opposite the hotel, and I would stay in the car watching the waves while he had a quick drink with his mates. Driving to the airport to watch planes take off was another favourite activity, and later, in my preteen years, I went with him to baseball and soccer games—all non-traditional pastimes for middle-class girls of my age in the 1950s.

## Mother and Daughter

Having been born when my parents were older and had some savings, I was sent to a private school. From 1947 to 1960, I attended a prestigious, but at that time relatively inexpensive, girls' school, Kambala Church of England Foundation School for Girls, in Rose Bay, the suburb adjacent to Vaucluse where I grew up. My mother's health had been poor for several years following surgery in 1934 for appendicitis and in 1947 for gallstones. An emergency hospitalization in February 1948 prevented her from seeing me leave for my first day of school, a disappointment that she never forgot, although my father took me to visit her, in my brand new school uniform, that afternoon. Given her health problems, she wanted me to be able to travel to and from school by myself as soon as I was old enough. It seemed to be taken for granted that my father, despite being retired, could not be expected to drive or escort me to school every day. With Kambala conveniently located on the tram route, my mother would see me off in the mornings and watch for me in the afternoons. When I reached school, a police officer, usually a woman, was always on duty to escort groups of girls across the busy street, and eventually traffic lights were installed.

According to head mistress Fifi Hawthorne's account, Kambala's fees in 1947 were "considerably less than those of other schools of comparable standing"; they ranged from 5 guineas (5 pounds, 5 shillings) to 12 guineas (12 pounds, 12 shillings) per year, depending on the child's age (Hawthorne, 1972: 159). Fees in 1948 at a comparable private girls' school, Abbotsleigh, started at 7 guineas, and by 1952 had almost doubled to 15 guineas (Burrows, 1968). The minimum (male) wage in the late 1940s was 6 pounds per week, so, in the unlikely event that a parent earning the lowest wage considered sending a daughter to Kambala, the year's fees would represent about one week's pay. Scholarships—three in number—were introduced in the 1930s; at this stage, the school population numbered about 100.

In 2000, Kambala's fees were $11,427, a figure that was typical of most private schools in Sydney (Baird and Noonan, 2000). One week's pay at the minimum wage today would cover only about two weeks' fees. Today's private schools are largely attended by the children of the wealthy and by a small number of scholarship recipients. About seven scholarships are offered at Kambala, although the school population now exceeds 600. In other words, the Kambala of the 1950s was a significantly different school than it had become by the end of the century. Interestingly, in 2003, the *Sydney Morning Herald* viewed as newsworthy a story about a Kambala graduate who became a bus driver at the age of 36. However, since her first career had been teaching English to overseas students, her middle-class credentials were established (Davis, 2003).

Carolyn Steedman's reflections on social class—"One hundred years ago, I'd have been cleaning your shoes"—resonate with my own. As a child playing on the verandah of Tivoli, the original 1834 Kambala building, I was standing on sandstone slabs laid by

# "... A BAD START IN MY LIFE BUT A HAPPY ENDING"

convicts, one of whom could easily have been my great-grandfather. Another sandstone mansion, Vaucluse House, which Titus Evers had in fact helped to build, was about half a mile away from Kambala.

I found a closer connection, chronologically and symbolically, in Miss Hawthorne's history of Kambala (1972: 68). She recorded that, in 1921, the proceeds from a school concert, organized "to raise funds for worthy causes," had been given to the Sydney Girls' Friendly Society Hostel (GFS). On April 7 of that same year, a 22-year-old factory worker, Margaret Evers, my mother, moved into this hostel.

The GFS had been established by the Anglican Church in England in 1875 and introduced to Australia in 1879 to provide accommodation and training to working-class girls and young women, as well as some level of surveillance. The Victorian branch, established in 1881, sought "to maintain among girls a high ideal of moral character and to preserve in the paths of virtue those who are entering on the business of life" by offering "wholesome amusement" along with cooking and "house management" classes (cited in Finch, 1990). Sarah McCallum apparently shared the same views on the threat to a girl's "virtue" posed by urban life, as Margaret explained:

> My grandma did not believe me when I told her I had to work back at night so she made me come home for my tea and one night she sent a lady friend back to work with me and then she found out I did work back at night.

For my mother, GFS housing represented a considerable improvement on her grandmother's boarding house and her other inner-suburban accommodation, although she hardly needed instruction in housework after her childhood apprenticeship. She had moved several times in the period 1918–1920, first living in Lidcombe with her sister Doris and husband Sam, then in a small town west of Sydney as a mother's helper, then back to the inner suburbs.

> I got board at Annandale with a couple and their child. I had to share my room with the wife. I did not stop there long, then moved to Stanmore, not a bad place but the lady bred dogs, it was alright until she made jam in the copper after boiling all the dogs' towels in the copper.
>
> In 1921, I moved to the Girls' Friendly Society opposite the University. There were about 40 girls there, we certainly had fun. I shared a room with four but I only used the room for dressing as our beds were on an open verandah. I used to put another mattress on top to keep warm.
>
> This was the first time I had running water in the bathroom. In Grandma's house you used to carry buckets of water from the copper. She had to economize.

## Teaching/Learning How to Be a Woman

My mother didn't view men or marriage as women's *raison d'être*. I was quite young when she began advising me not to marry until I was well into my 20s, and to travel and see the world before I became "tied down" with a husband and children. Unfamiliar with post-secondary education and professional careers for women, neither parent encouraged me in that direction. In fact, when we went to Sydney University's open house when I was about 14, my mother commented, "Well, this is probably as close as you'll get to a university." She was not opposed to further education or careers for women; rather, the university was outside her frame of reference until I began undergraduate studies at age 29, and I was the only member of my family on my mother's side to complete a doctorate. When I did so, she was very pleased, but expressed the hope that I was not going to "do any more university degrees."

Regarding human reproduction, my mother said very little except to explain menstrual periods and to observe, in passing, that "men can be brutes," leaving the rest to my imagination. I could see no reason for celebrating the onset of menstruation. A school friend's rationale—"it's good because it means you can have a baby"—left me unmoved and cynical at age 13. "Who wants a baby?" I thought. In senior school biology classes, we were introduced to reproduction in frogs, followed by mammals and humans, with Miss Cockburn's dry delivery focusing exclusively on anatomy and physiology. Typical of the era, both the curriculum and the teachers who presented it were silent on the social and emotional aspects of human sexuality, although various myths and facts circulated among my peers.

Having heard no message to the contrary, I reached adolescence believing that marriage was a choice, not a destiny, and I didn't view childless women as incomplete or unfulfilled. Numerous family friends—women whom I called "Auntie"—were married and childless, or unmarried, childless, and living with family or friends. I heard a few references to "old maids," but since sexuality was not a topic to be discussed in front of a young girl, I received no other details. Furthermore, most of my teachers were unmarried women (although, as I discovered later, some had lived in lesbian partnerships for many years). Imagine my horror at the age of 12 when a classmate pronounced unequivocally, "Everyone gets married." There was a clear consensus among my peers on this question. I was so outraged that I had a wager with a friend that, 10 years from then, I would not be married. I was wrong; I got married at 22, and by 25, had two children. Ironically, I happened to see this friend the day after my wedding, after having lost touch with her when she had changed schools six years earlier, but neither of us remembered the wager. In short, despite my mother's messages to the contrary, I was at that time a fairly typical product of heterosexualizing influences. To be valued and needed, the Australian adolescent girl of the 1950s aspired to become a wife and mother.

## Teaching/Learning the Value of Money

One of the most obvious legacies of my parents' working-class roots concerned financial matters. Typical of arrangements in working-class marriages, my mother's weekly housekeeping money was doled out by my father. She had little discretionary spending money—mostly leftovers from the grocery money—and only a small bank account of her own until she reached 65, when she qualified for what was then called the old age pension. I learned the lesson that money was to be saved, or to be spent carefully after due consideration. My mother's early training in frugal housekeeping was reflected in many money-saving habits that I assumed all mothers practised: using her sewing and knitting skills to make clothes and household items; turning over my father's worn shirt collars; making hand towels out of old bath towels; cutting worn sheets in half and rejoining them so that the unworn areas were in the middle; using washable sanitary pads (a practice that I quickly rejected as a teenager); and buying children's clothing several sizes too large, then putting hems, tucks, and pleats in appropriate places. In the same recycling vein, my father used the lumber from packing crates to make wardrobes and cupboards, and collected manure left on the street by the milkman's horse for the garden.

In the upper middle-class milieu of Kambala, I was one of the few girls who wore a "second-hand" uniform, used a "second-hand" tennis racquet, and had a father who did not have a white-collar occupation. Worse still, many people assumed my parents were my grandparents. I discovered many years later that they were not much older than parents of some of my friends. My mother, however, was less fashionably and expensively dressed than their mothers, and she rarely wore makeup. Furthermore, as a woman who began her apprenticeship in housework at age five and suffered several years of ill health, my mother had aged more visibly than her healthier upper-class counterparts. However, she was in her 100th year when she died, and had two sisters who lived past 100. The Evers family demonstrated that longevity is not only dependent on socio-economic status. Despite economic hardships during childhood, and in some instances throughout their entire lives, my mother and most of her siblings lived into their 80s and 90s, and her two sisters lived past 100 years of age.

## Conclusion

Returning to my earlier thoughts on the ways that women imagine their lives and the impacts of social and political change, I can identify several crossroads in my mother's life: the four-year-old country girl leaving her family behind to take up training in "housework" at the hands of a strict disciplinarian grandmother; the bright adolescent forced to leave school and earn a living; the young woman considering an offer of marriage from an older man; and the middle-aged woman discovering that she is pregnant again. All these events took place in a social context in which women and children, particularly those of the working class, were vulnerable to exploitation and abuse at home and in the workplace, with little or no legislative protection. Margaret was dependent on her husband for financial security, and, as a middle-aged woman with no training, few employable skills, and a young child, she had limited options if she left the marriage.

In my own case, the crossroads in childhood and adolescence were relatively benign: my parents' choice of Kambala for my schooling, and the joint decision that I would go to teachers' college. By the 1960s, with the provision of scholarships and changing societal attitudes, post-secondary education was within the reach of many young women who in earlier generations would have left school to enter the workforce, as the next chapter will demonstrate.

CHAPTER 2

# "A Place of Sound Discipline": Kambala Foundation School for Girls

For over a century, Australian non-government education has, in broad terms, followed long-standing British trends and traditions, with the children of the upper middle and ruling classes usually enrolled in private schools. Non-government schools were originally termed "private" or "independent," since it was not until the 1970s that they began to receive state and Commonwealth government grants. In the case of Catholic schools, these funds accounted for 58 percent of their income in 1977, while for Anglican schools, the figure was 21 percent (Schools Commission statistics cited in Hogan, 1984: 108.)

Unlike the educational system in Canada and the United States, Australia's non-government schools, predominantly Anglican and Roman Catholic, attracted a significant proportion of students. Over the period 1905–1980, between 18.9 and 24.1 percent of students attended non-government schools, which, in the last two decades of that period, numbered approximately 2,500 (Hogan, 1984: 49, 57). As early as 1900, Sydney had eight private girls' schools, most of which survived competition from the publicly funded system and continue to operate into the 21st century.

## Learning One's Station in Life

Australia's free, secular, and compulsory education Acts of the late 1800s resulted in "a hardening of middle class attitudes against the publicly funded schools," with prosperous parents increasingly viewing the private girls' school as a refuge from "the contaminating influence of the state school child" (Kyle, 1986: 109). In other words, an unintended outcome of universal, publicly funded education was the entrenching of social class differences. Eighty years later, Bob Connell and his colleagues (1982) presented research evidence demonstrating that the publicly funded system in Australia was, in fact, a working-class school system.

Australian historian Judith Gill (1995) interviewed 11 out of an original class of 12 students who had graduated from a Melbourne Catholic girls' school in 1958. This was a cohort with similar experiences to my own; I attended Kambala from 1947 to 1960. These Catholic students had endured a somewhat more repressive school climate than their counterparts in Anglican schools, although there were some shared experiences. Given the generally lower fees imposed by Catholic schools, Gill's participants were "daughters of the newly aspiring lower middle class," whereas most Kambala girls were daughters of the middle and upper classes. None of the parents of Gill's sample had completed university, whereas at Kambala there was an abundance of fathers in the professions, most notably doctors and lawyers. As the daughter of a builder, I was a member of a small minority in terms of both my father's occupation and social capital.

Gill presented an insightful analysis of the memories and feelings expressed by the women in her study. She reported that, although these well-educated women were now in their 50s, they had not developed a class analysis of their own schooling, or of the educational system in general. Instead, they focused on individual experiences and perceptions of the school as a meritocracy. She summarized their reflections as follows:

> ... the determined location of self-as-individual, which can be seen as directly flowing from the educational style of the time, precludes a vision of the school's function to serve the upwardly aspiring social group. Society was/is somehow "out there" and the task for us as individuals is to devote ourselves to the interests of right and proper behaviour, rather than analyse our school's place within that social division. (Gill, 1995: 9)

Having what Gill called a "blinkered" vision of the world, these women evaluated gender issues on an individual basis, and expressed their hostility to and rejection of the feminist movement. However, Australian Catholic schools have produced feminists, Germaine Greer being one of the first and most prominent internationally.

Although they were critical of many aspects of their schooling, Gill's participants still displayed loyalty and school spirit as if, in her words, "they maintained some investment in the self that had been produced through their experience of schooling" (Gill, 1995: 8). Many published autobiographical accounts, as well as my own story, share some of this ambivalence, prompted not necessarily or solely by feelings of loyalty, but rather by the need to reflect on one's school days in a more nuanced way, and to examine the contradictions rather than to offer blanket criticism. Like the Melbourne students, Kambala's "old girls" (the traditional term still used in Australia to denote alumnae of private girls' schools) vividly recall the best and the worst teachers: the ones who embodied the narrowest pedagogical and disciplinary approaches of the postwar years, and the others whose genuine commitment to teaching, rather than commitment to the headmistress, opened our minds to new ways of thinking. Teachers ranged from quiet and ineffective to authoritarian and rigid, and only a small number combined excellent teaching skills with warm personalities. Although Kambala was a private school, and therefore viewed as offering superior instruction, the student-teacher ratio in junior school was remarkably high by today's standards: 38 in second class (grade 2), 35 in fourth class, and 39 in fifth class, according to my school reports from the 1950s. Clearly, ideas of individualized teaching and smaller class size had not yet been put into practice.

Many of those who succeeded in Kambala's classrooms in the 1950s acknowledge the flawed system of private education for girls in that era, but at the same time value the ways in which the school's unequivocal emphasis on academic achievement served us in our subsequent lives and careers. Conversely, many of those who "failed" by Kambala's definition look back on their schooling with bitterness, and point to their later educational and workplace achievements in order to demonstrate that they have succeeded despite having been labelled "dumb" or "bad" at school.

Jill Ker Conway, vice president of the University of Toronto in the 1970s and later president of Smith College, wrote of her experiences in two private girls' schools in Sydney in the first of her autobiographical works, *The Road from Coorain* (1990). Born and raised on a sheep station in the outback of NSW, Conway had difficulty adjusting to life at Queenwood and Abbotsleigh schools. Although her years as a boarder at Abbotsleigh were marked, with a few exceptions, by more benign leadership and more progressive pedagogy than her Kambala counterparts experienced, both schools used the same rigid rules on matters of "ladylike" behaviour and comportment. Moreover, both catered to a social elite—"privileged girls and young women who had an obligation to represent the best standards of behaviour to the world at large" (Conway, 1990: 102). These were girls who were "born to be leaders," but, as Conway observed, the schools of this era conveyed confusing messages about girls' destinies.

> ... the precise nature of the leadership was by no means clear. For some of our mentors, excelling meant a fashionable marriage and leadership in philanthropy. For others, it meant intellectual achievement and aspiration to a university degree. Since the great majority of the parents ... supported the first definition, the question of the social values which should inform leadership was carefully glossed over. (Conway, 1990: 102)

As liberal feminists have subsequently argued, girls' schools provided female teachers with secure career paths and gave girls the opportunity to see positive examples of female competence, leadership, and academic achievement. For example, the notion of girls' "math anxiety" had no currency at Kambala; some girls were good at the subject, while some were not, but we were never led to believe that being female meant we couldn't or shouldn't excel at mathematics. Similarly, with the exception of the external Leaving Certificate examination, there were no situations when our achievements as girls were compared unfavourably to those of boys. Outside of school, being "brainy" was not an asset in terms of one's popularity with boys, nor was it necessarily a liability.

Like other private girls' schools in the 1950s, Kambala's notion of service to others reinforced rather than challenged colonialist and classist thinking about cultural and socio-economic differences. By learning *our* "station in life," we were also learning the standing of *others*. Of course, such lessons were not universally accepted by graduates of private schools, some of whom applied their formidable intellects and political astuteness to the task of transforming society through feminist activism. Author Robin Davidson characterized Australia's brand of sexism and some of its outcomes as follows:

> Contemporary Australia has a reputation for producing tough-minded women. Indeed, tough-minded women are one of our principal exports. In a culture where misogyny has deep historical roots ... it is only to be expected that daughters of fifties' mothers should have produced an Antipodean feminism with a sharp cutting edge. (Davidson, 1987: 179)

## "An Ability to Control": Miss Fifi Hawthorne

Miss Fifi Hawthorne was headmistress of Kambala from 1933 to 1966, and in 1968 she was requested by the Old Girls' Union to write an official history to mark the school's upcoming 85th anniversary.[1] The book is largely a factual and uncritical account of events and achievements, and she devoted about 60 percent of the book's content to a chronicle of her own 33 years at the helm.

Miss Hawthorne's account of events in 1930 and 1931, based on archival sources, included a reference to the fact that private school enrolments were hit "rather heavily" by the Depression and teachers "all agreed to a cut in their salaries" (1972: 100). Domestic staff wages were also cut, with some receiving less than 30 shillings per week, presumably in addition to room and board, while teaching staff faced a 10 percent reduction (Nobbs, 1987: 71). The notion that female teachers had a choice when Kambala Council, replete with powerful and privileged men, requested their *agreement* to this cut was flawed. In Nadia Wheatley's critical analysis of the impact of the Depression on workers in Sydney's eastern suburbs, she included examples such as the Kambala teachers' pay cuts, the sacking of four masters at Cranbrook boys' school, and wealthy families' practice of replacing live-in domestic staff with casuals (Wheatley, 1988: 211).

From her school management perspective, Miss Hawthorne often wrote about the difficulties of retaining "good help" for domestic work, particularly during World War II. One of her solutions was to train the girls who boarded to clear tables and push trolleys into the pantry after meals, and occasionally to dry dishes or sweep dormitories. She had little patience with boarders who had been accustomed to servants: learning the hard way, she asserted, "was good for their souls!" (Hawthorne, 1972: 147). However, by the postwar period, Miss Hawthorne was agreeing with other Australian headmistresses that it was unfair to require teaching staff to supervise boarders' domestic duties. To alleviate the problem in the 1950s, she allowed domestic staff to use their bedrooms and the school kitchen over the summer holidays, rather than having to find alternative work and accommodation for two months (Hawthorne, 1972: 174–175).

In the more personal sections of her book, Miss Hawthorne acknowledged the support of "loyal" staff members, praised the efforts of successful pupils, and glossed over those whose careers at Kambala were short and nasty. However, to my eyes, the overall tone was surprisingly humble and generous, given her authoritarian leadership style.

Despite her general avoidance of controversial topics, she made reference to four failures in the 1953 Intermediate Certificate (third-year high school) examinations, and proceeded to blame these girls for "laziness rather than inability." Citing the negative effects of current societal trends, she wrote:

> We had found that the wireless, motion pictures during the week, parties or dances with thoughts about clothes and partners weeks before were somewhat of a distraction to the under sixteens. This was the beginning of the "emancipation" of the very young. (Hawthorne, 1972: 191)

Her oblique reference to girls' "thoughts" about "partners" obviously meant their preoccupation with boyfriends. Outside of school, most Kambala girls in early and mid-adolescence were typical products of 1950s socialization into heterosexual femininity. Girls who gave priority to other pursuits, academic or athletic, and even those who later came out as lesbian, were unlikely to mount any public challenge to the prevailing heterosexual norms of middle-class and ruling-class culture.

In 1954, Miss Hawthorne commented on a slightly different problem occurring among 10-year-old children:

> There had been a considerable number of birthday parties to which every member of the class ... had been invited. In some cases every guest was given a present, in others the entertainment was very lavish. (Hawthorne, 1972: 195)

These parties had been popular among some of my peers in junior school. Parents rented facilities usually reserved for adult celebrations, hired magicians or puppeteers, and distributed expensive gifts to every girl. Other birthday parties were held in large, lavishly furnished private homes that reflected the social and financial status of the girl's family, since, from a young age, we were aware of visible markers of wealth. Some of these houses were inherited after parents died and became home to the next generation of Kambala girls in a pattern that demonstrated the predictable reproduction of social class.

It appears that Miss Hawthorne and other teachers were concerned about ostentatious displays of wealth and party activities inappropriate to the age group. This issue and related problems of parties and dances attended by affluent senior students were discussed by heads of six private schools in the eastern suburbs, and, according to Miss Hawthorne's account, a letter representing the views of the three male and three female principals was distributed to all students. I have no personal memory of this, probably because the letter was mailed to my parents, who did not discuss it with me. Miss Hawthorne reported that the letter was favourably received by many parents. It included suggestions for invitations, supervision, behaviour, dress, escorts, and refreshment, and reiterated the schools' position in relation to school dances—they should be semi-formal, chaperoned, alcohol free, with invitations issued by the school. In short, these heterosexual courtship rituals were encouraged as long as they were controlled by the school.

A few years earlier, the unnamed author (a teacher, possibly Molly Ainsworth) of an unpublished editorial intended for the 1951 issue of the *Kambala Chronicle* had also been critical of what she viewed as negative postwar impacts:

> ... the present generation of girls has grown up during the war and is now sharing in the general reluctance to work, which always seems to follow a war. There is not now the same intimacy between girls and staff, nor the same eagerness for and interest in work which was evident in previous years. This is partly balanced, however, by the enormous enthusiasm for sport amongst all classes. (Editorial, 1951)

Although this editorial writer noted the key role of a school magazine in communication and community building—an "integral part of school life," in her words—the *Kambala Chronicle* ceased publication in 1939 due to wartime shortages of materials, and defied attempts to revive it in the late 1940s and 1950s. A complete handwritten, unpublished draft was produced in 1951, but it was not until 1967, the year following Miss Hawthorne's retirement, that the newly named *School Magazine* finally appeared.

Mollie Ainsworth, mathematics teacher since the 1930s, wrote a glowing tribute to Miss Hawthorne in the introduction to *Kambala: A History*, praising her "qualities of leadership and quiet efficiency" and her key role in shaping the school's reputation as "a place of sound discipline and good academic achievement." She noted "a relaxation of standards generally" in the postwar years, but assured the reader that Miss Hawthorne had maintained and personally exemplified the ideals of "self-discipline, dedication, compassion [and] good manners" for all Kambala girls (Ainsworth, 1972).

Among many of my contemporaries in the 1950s, "quietly efficient" and "compassionate" were not the terms we would have chosen to describe the headmistress. Generations of girls, myself included, shared perceptions of a strict disciplinarian, prone to unpredictable outbursts and capable of reducing students or staff to tears. This is not to suggest that Miss Hawthorne was atypical of that era. Jill Ker Conway, for example, described the vice principal of Abbotsleigh, another private girls' school, in similar terms (Conway, 1990: 113). Anecdotal evidence and my own personal experience also support the claim that, in the 1950s and 1960s, many women in leadership positions in all-female institutions—most notably, girls' private schools, Sydney Kindergarten Training College, and hospital-based nursing schools—exercised their power in equally authoritarian ways.

It is possible that the Kambala girls who were boarders saw Miss Hawthorne's warmer side, and her account showed that she held cherished memories of her role *in loco parentis* in the boarding house, particularly when she faced the challenge of protecting her charges during World War II. In a sense, the boarders and the resident teachers constituted her "family" and Kambala was their "home." After her retirement, most old girls who saw her at reunions found her a non-threatening person, "just a little old lady" who was genuinely interested in our lives, families, and achievements. I visited her in 1984 at her home and we had a lively conversation about my university studies and the old girls of my generation with whom she kept in touch. I knew that she had been disappointed when I chose teachers' college rather than university after leaving school in 1960, and I wanted to tell her that I'd completed my doctorate and written a book about women and sport.

Former Kambala pupil, Penny Nelson, provided an apt first impression of Miss Hawthorne:

> ... an imposing woman who wore a black gown over her sober, tailored clothes, and pulled her hair back in a plaited bun. My mother seemed in awe of her at our first interview; there was something about the piercing blue eyes and severe clothing that signalled disapproval of anything unauthorized or frivolous. (Nelson, 1995: 36)

The only teacher who routinely wore an academic gown and wrote "B.A." after her signature on students' reports, Miss Hawthorne was highly visible as both university graduate and headmistress. Other teachers wore their gowns only on prize-giving day, the one occasion when girls could determine which teachers had university degrees. More visible recognition of university credentials, perhaps through the wearing of gowns for morning assemblies, would have served as a positive example and inspiration to Kambala girls, many of whom had no female family members or friends with these qualifications. However, the hierarchy symbolized by Miss Hawthorne's black gown was well entrenched by the 1950s.

In her account, Miss Hawthorne reported that former students visiting the school in 1958 reminisced about her drawing room, where the initial interviews were always held. These women still found that the room had "an awe-inspiring atmosphere. Even now when they were in their twenties, thirties or even forties, they still felt they should enter it on tiptoe!" (Hawthorne, 1972: 211–212). She seemed to find their reaction more amusing than alarming. In fact, the incident may have earned a place in the book simply because it demonstrated that knowing one's place had been thoroughly absorbed by many generations of girls during her leadership.

Jill Ker Conway, at age 11, had a markedly different experience with Abbotsleigh's headmistress. Impressed with Conway's vocabulary and creative mind, Miss Everitt had "cheerfully ignored the admission rules" that gave preference to daughters of old girls, and immediately admitted her to the school (Conway, 1990: 97). Although I don't remember all the details, my mother often told me what transpired at our initial interview. Dressed in my best clothes, I had demonstrated, upon request, that I could recite the alphabet and count to 10 (or perhaps it was 20) and Miss Hawthorne had commented that I "looked intelligent." That vote of confidence, along with my parents' ability to pay the fees, seemed to constitute the admission requirements in my case.

On the question of admission to Kambala, the school archives held a letter dated May 1948 that Miss Hawthorne had received from a Mrs. Eleanor Newton, of Culcairn, in rural NSW, writing on behalf of her friend Mrs. John Barker. After establishing her own credentials as the former Nell Abbott, "daughter of the late Sir Joseph Abbott," and a Kambala old girl, Mrs. Newton wrote:

> I do hope that you will be able to find a place for Janice [Barker] as she is a particularly nice little girl and should do well at school. Her father's people the Barkers, of course are very well known as sportsmen. Her great uncle Nigel Barker being an Olympic Games representative & her father while at St. Pauls was captain of the University Rugby team. (Newton, 1948)

Interestingly, the reference to (male) family members' sporting achievement was seen as a way of strengthening the girl's application. Even though Eleanor Newton had not herself been a pupil during the Hawthorne years, she seems to have been aware of the current headmistress's emphasis on sport.

The school's 100th anniversary in 1987 saw the publication of a second official history, *Kambala: The First Hundred Years 1887–1987*, compiled by one of my contemporaries, Alanna Nobbs, an old girl who was at that time a senior lecturer in ancient history at Macquarie University. Despite her background as an historian, Nobbs's account of the Hawthorne years, in chapters entitled "Energy and Expansion, 1933–1949" and "The Years of Stability, 1950–1984," gives no critical analysis of the school, its teachers, or, most significantly, its headmistress. The index subentries under "Miss Hawthorne, Fifi" speak for themselves: "achievements of; administrative talents of; ... dedication and energy of; ... educational philosophy and innovations of; ... pupils' affection for; tributes to" (Nobbs, 1987: 242–243). Admittedly, the Kambala Centenary History Committee that commissioned the work was composed of old girls, Council members, and teachers—men and women unlikely to allow a critical analysis to be published. And, while educational historians such as Martin Crotty (2003) can draw on a large number of memoirs that document the experiences of private schoolboys in Australia—nine in the case of Melbourne's Scotch College alone—there is not the same wealth of stories written by former private schoolgirls.

On the occasion of Miss Hawthorne's retirement, the School Council's secretary, Roy Cox, echoed Nobbs's sentiments: "Miss Hawthorne brought to her task a tireless energy, inspiring teaching, a passion for tidiness, a love of girls and an ability to control girls and staff, at the same time having their respect and love" (cited in Nobbs, 1987: 133). In these days of more democratic school management styles and more egalitarian relationships between principals and teachers, as well as private school teachers' unionized status through the Independent Teachers' Federation, Miss Hawthorne's "ability to control" staff would not necessarily be seen as a positive attribute. However, I doubt that anyone would have questioned her dedication to her work. For example, her teaching responsibilities included Latin, and during one winter term in 1958, she was absent for a week or more with the flu. Concerned that the senior Latin students would fall behind in the syllabus, she invited this small group of girls to her flat, which was attached to the senior school, and conducted the class there. Of course, reputations—hers and the school's—were at stake; in her first 13 years of teaching Latin, no girl had ever failed a public exam (Hawthorne, 1972: 155).

Mollie Ainsworth is correct, too, in stating that Miss Hawthorne inspired loyalty among her staff of "able, dedicated" teachers, whose long records of service provide ample evidence of this claim. When I talked to Mollie years later, it was clear that she saw Miss Hawthorne as symbolic of Kambala's "Golden Age," and she, together with several other older teachers, retired shortly after Miss Hawthorne left.

Another long-serving teacher, Miss Florence Burgess, spent almost 40 years at Kambala. In Miss Hawthorne's assessment, "Her loyalty to Kambala, her strong sense of duty, her Christian way of living made her a valued teacher" (Hawthorne, 1972: 196). Nobbs (1987: 112) endorsed this view, as well as commending Miss Burgess for the "thorough grounding" in the basics that she imparted to the girls in third class. Both official histories glossed over the fact that Miss Burgess was the only teacher in the school who routinely, and with apparent impunity, meted out corporal punishment. She would line up offenders at the front of the class and hit them on the palm of the hand with a wooden ruler for offences ranging from talking in class to untidy handwriting. No other teacher, not even the headmistress, disciplined students this way, so it would appear to have contravened school policy.

Privately, my cohort at Kambala used to mock Miss Hawthorne's outbursts and inflexibility. We became accustomed to hearing that we were "the worst class ever" and we came to expect the standard response "It's never been done before" whenever a change in program, curriculum, or uniform was suggested. Ironically, the major external impetus for curricular change—the Wyndham Report, which required four sciences courses and extended high school by one year—came into effect just before her retirement, and she had no choice but to adapt. As she noted without further comment in her annual report for 1963, "The syllabuses for Science (which involved Physics, Chemistry, Biology and Geology) and Mathematics *revolutionized* our timetable" (Hawthorne, 1972: 227, emphasis added).

## The Making of the Ruling Class

The ways in which Australian private schools created and entrenched social class and ethnic divisions have been extensively documented (Anderson, 1990; Connell et al., 1982; Kyle, 1986; McCalman, 1993; McGregor, 2001; Teese, 1998; Theobald, 1996). This is not to suggest, however, that there is a straightforward reproduction of power and privilege through education. As Bob Connell and his colleagues found in their study of publicly funded and independent schools in Sydney and Adelaide, instances of upward or downward mobility do occur, students resist class-based ideologies, elite private girls' schools challenge ruling-class patriarchy, and such schools "can be the vehicle for significant *changes* in established social relationships" (Connell et al., 1982: 190, emphasis in original).

Sociologist Craig McGregor and others have argued that, despite the rhetoric that Australia is a "classless society," there are four clear class divisions: the underclass, working class, middle class, and upper class (which Connell et al. termed "ruling class"). Members of the underclass are typically Aboriginal, ethnic minorities, or poor White. Not coincidentally, Australians who occupy the middle and upper classes have predominantly British Protestant origins, while Catholics (more so than those of other religions) represent a larger proportion of working-class people (McGregor, 2001: 263). Private Catholic schools, with a few notable exceptions, charged significantly lower fees than their Protestant counterparts, partly because they received higher government subsidies.

On the question of visible class distinctions, McGregor was exaggerating only slightly when he characterized an upper-class woman as

> [a] society matron with a fruity voice from Toorak or Vaucluse whose life seems to revolve around charity galas/fashion openings/holidays in Europe/operating a trust fund for the school Old Girls, and whose husband is not only a multimillionaire but is an office holder in the Liberal [conservative] Party and a director of several companies ... (McGregor, 2001: 243)

Until the 1970s or later, Australian daily newspapers regularly included "Social Pages" with news and photographs of upper-class (and occasionally middle-class) women's busy social calendars. Penny Nelson's mother, Micky McNicoll, was responsible for the *Daily Telegraph*'s women's pages, the contents of which Penny aptly characterized as follows:

> Sunbaking on the beach are Mr. and Mrs. Malename Surname. They alternate between their Palm Beach house and their lovely cruiser, *J'attendrai*, moored in Pittwater. (Nelson, 1995: 59)

Mr. and Mrs. Malename Surname's daughters were probably pupils at a private school like Kambala—girls who would grow up to become McGregor's "society matrons."

As McGregor went on to explain, gender as well as class differences are evident at all levels of education, with the position of the rural and business elite secured in part through the private school education of their sons, and, in recent decades, their daughters. Historian Janet McCalman reported similar patterns: "The traditional middle class frame of mind depended on a sense of personal righteousness—of believing oneself to be deserving, that one's life comforts and social position had been legitimately earned" (McCalman, 1993: 300).

McGregor, who had attended Cranbrook in the 1940s as a scholarship boy from rural NSW, had an insider's view of a private boys' school. Although "displays of wealth were not only discouraged but prohibited ... [and] the only outsiders were Jews and the sons of Asian diplomats," he recalled that snobbery and arrogance directed at working-class people, especially striking trade unionists, "Commos," and members of the Labour Party were rampant. Cranbrook boys "were continually being told that we were the nation's future leaders ... and that the school expected us to achieve positions of distinction and influence" (McGregor, 2001: 132, 133). Meanwhile, a few miles further east along New South Head Road, Rose Bay, Kambala girls were rarely exposed to such inspirational rhetoric, and most would have been hard pressed to name a trade union leader or a politician. In that era, Kambala teachers rarely discussed public affairs or encouraged girls to read the newspapers, and television was not common in Sydney homes until the late 1950s. Daughters of the middle and ruling classes, or, more specifically, the academic stream, received mixed messages about the school's expectations and aspirations for them: an undergraduate university education in arts or humanities, a short career, and then marriage.

## Noblesse Oblige

McGregor described the function of contemporary private education in the following way:

> Private schools ... set out quite openly to provide a different education for upper-class pupils and to emphasize the distance between them and students at other schools ( ... hats, blazers, uniforms, school songs, speech days and so on are emblems of this); they stress leadership, academic success, discipline, and the importance of a career for both girls and boys; considerable attention is paid to good manners and style. There is no doubt ... that they are providing a "superior" education to "superior" people. (McGregor, 2001: 292)

Admittedly, public school students wore uniforms as well, but there were some unique aspects of the private school outfits—gloves, crests, and hats, for example, as well as the expensive price tag—that distinguished them from the others.

The so-called "superior" students, particularly girls in Anglican schools, were taught the noblesse oblige ethos and the importance of Christian charity. This must have presented teachers with a challenge in the 1930s when, according to the *Kambala Chronicle*, many privileged old girls were heading for finishing schools in Europe and debuts in London (Wheatley, 1988: 220).

In a 1934 *Kambala Chronicle* editorial, Miss Hawthorne identified the key functions of a Church school as "service for others and a deepening of our spiritual life" (cited in Nobbs, 1987: 80). Her annual report dutifully noted girls' fundraising efforts for charities: the Friday collection of one penny from every girl, and the concerts and social functions organized in conjunction with the Old Girls' Union. The practice of making an annual donation to the Ashfield

Infants' Home, at that time a home for orphans and abused children, was established in 1907, and, in one of the many examples of Kambala traditions, donations to this organization continued throughout the century. Ashfield Infants' Home, however, changed with the times, and in the 1970s was the first to move from residential care to family daycare.

Other beneficiaries of the Friday pennies included the Bush Brothers (missionaries in outback Australia), the Australian Board of Missions, the Barnardo Homes, and overseas Christian missions. Guest speakers from these organizations would visit the school regularly to raise girls' awareness that there were children and adults "less fortunate" than ourselves—Aboriginal or Chinese people, for example, who needed the Christian gospel for salvation of their souls, so we were led to believe. As the next chapter will show, Kambala girls of the 1950s experienced complex and often contradictory messages about gender, achievement, and Christian responsibilities.

CHAPTER 3

# Kambala: Learning to Win, Learning to Lose

In the 1950s and 1960s, as now, most Australians could readily rank the relative prestige of various suburbs and various occupations (McGregor, 2001: 155). This awareness was well developed among Kambala girls in the 1950s. From a young age, we knew that families who owned houses were wealthier than those who rented flats, and we accurately ranked Rose Bay and Vaucluse as more desirable and prestigious suburbs than Bondi Beach or Bondi Junction.

## Defining Moments and Australian Accents

Penny Nelson (1995: 41) remembered a Kambala teacher asking each girl about her father's occupation, presumably for the school records (although I don't recall that we were given an explanation at the time). Penny particularly admired the sangfroid of one girl, Jill, who calmly announced that her father was a funeral director, in a context where prestige accrued only to doctors, lawyers, accountants, clergy, and other professional men.

When my turn came, I struggled with the question. At age eight, I didn't understand the concept of retirement, although I knew my father did not go out to work every day. Then I remembered what I had recently observed him doing in his workshop, and so I announced that he mended hot water heaters. When I told my parents at the dinner table, I received a shocked response, along with some coaching. In future, I was to say that my father was a property owner, since he owned two blocks of flats that he had built in the 1940s. However, whenever I visited friends' houses to play or to attend a birthday party, it was clear their fathers did not have workshops or wear overalls around the house.

Years later, a similar problem surfaced when, as fifth-year students (aged 17), we were asked to provide the name and address of the boy with whom we would attend the semi-formal graduation dance, so that the school could issue the invitations. My date was not a private school boy; he worked as a lowly office clerk and lived in Bondi Junction. Although Kambala had instilled some class consciousness, I tended to go out with public rather than private school boys. In this case, I pondered whether an invitation addressed to Waverley—the correct municipality, but not his correct postal address—would reach him by mail, because to admit that he lived in Bondi Junction was to advertise that he was a working-class boy. I cannot remember how I resolved the problem, but hindsight tells me it would not have mattered. Both the headmistress and my peers would have spotted his working-class origins as soon as they heard him speak.

Broad Australian, as linguists call it, is the typically working-class accent characterized in popular culture by Paul Hogan as Crocodile Dundee and Barry Humphries as Dame Edna. Most middle-class people—accounting for about 55 percent of Australians—speak General Australian (McGregor, 2001: 161). A third style, termed the "Cultivated Accent," was modelled by news broadcasters on Australian Broadcasting Commission radio until the 1970s, and instilled into generations of upper-class children by traditional "elocution" teachers. A speaker of Broad Australian would have difficulty reproducing most vowel sounds to an elocution teacher's satisfaction. As a child, I learned that using long words at home would make adults laugh indulgently, while pronouncing some words the way I heard them at home would be corrected at school. My "accent problem" was not one of Broad versus General Australian, since my father, born and raised in Northumberland, in the north of England, retained his Geordie accent all his life, and my mother's brand of Australian was closer to General than Broad. Rather, it was a problem with the pronunciation of words that I had learned at home—like "engine" and "laundry"—and stubbornly continued to say incorrectly, according to standard middle-class Australian.

At home, especially for my father, my adolescent friendships and relationships with boys routinely generated conflict, but rarely because of social class differences, except on one occasion when he was not pleased to hear that I had walked home from the beach with two boys who worked as a builder's labourers. A member of the Master Builders' Association himself, my father understood the status hierarchy in the construction industry, and drew the line at his daughter socializing with a mere labourer.

As McGregor (2001: 158) explained, a "labour aristocracy" of skilled workers separated itself from the rest of the Australian working class on the basis of skill, education levels, craft union membership, and Anglo or Irish backgrounds. In the 1950s and 1960s, the trend toward skilled workers' self-identification as middle class was more marked in Australia than in American and British contexts, and my father usually followed this pattern. In good middle-class fashion, he voted Liberal rather than Labour, the party often characterized as "Commo" (Communist). For her part, my mother applied the label "common" to working-class women who allegedly flaunted their sexuality. At the same time, like other Australians with working-class origins, my parents deplored snobbery, affected accents, skiting (bragging), and ostentatious displays of wealth. Life was a balancing act between preserving some working-class loyalties and values, while guarding against revealing working-class roots when it was inappropriate or unwise to do so.

## High and Low Culture

In my experience of social studies up to the third year of high school, Australian history and geography, most notably White men's "discoveries," "conquests," and "taming" of the land, were covered, but women and Aboriginals were largely invisible. Australian content in the area of "high culture"—literature, poetry, art, drama, and music—was seriously lacking, and the literary canon was unequivocally British. Just as the private school uniform symbolized ties to the British Commonwealth in general, and the English private school system in particular, the curriculum downplayed the reality of our location on Australian soil, as if it were embarrassing to admit that we were standing, not "on England's green and pleasant fields," but on the red soil of a "sunburnt country."

In the Kambala context, "music" meant weekly singing classes in preparation for school concerts, classical piano, taught for additional fees by visiting music teachers, and a subject called "musical appreciation" wherein Miss Pritchard carried a portable phonograph and records to senior classes once a week, and played classical music for us to "appreciate." For their part, 1950s adolescents across social classes embraced popular culture, particularly rock music, and listening to radio "hit parades" while doing homework was a standard practice. At that time, local Australian rock musicians such as Col Joye, Lucky Starr, and Johnny O'Keefe—mostly young men with working-class roots—enjoyed considerable radio and television airtime.

At about age 15, I bought my first guitar, practised rock songs in front of the mirror, and successfully auditioned for a talent quest presented by Rumpus Room, a radio program geared to an adolescent audience. I chose to sing the rock version of "Rockabye Baby" out of a limited choice of songs played on Sydney radio stations, since most lyrics represented the male perspective. This kind of public engagement with popular culture was not common among Kambala girls. Only a few of my friends knew about my musical aspirations, which over the next few years took me to several, mostly unsuccessful, radio and television auditions.

Piano lessons taken at a younger age helped me to teach myself guitar chords, and so in a sense I was familiar with "high" as well as "low" culture. At age eight or nine, I had begged my parents to buy a piano and let me take lessons, and they eventually did so—a second-hand piano and lessons provided by the daughter of the local shoe repairman. Then, as now, my only classical aspiration was to play Chopin, and my preferences in popular music were folk and country. Some of my peers, as adolescents, attended Sydney Symphony Orchestra youth concerts and similar events, but high culture did not "take" in my case.

## Class, Gender, and Sexuality

Although social class differences and expectations were complex and changing, there was no ambiguity among Kambala girls when it came to dating. As one adolescent girl explained, her mother expected her to go out only with private schoolboys, the goal being for her to marry a doctor or a lawyer. Whenever we discussed boys, "What school does he go to?" was the first question asked. Having attended a private school in Brisbane in the 1950s and 1960s, author Robyn Davidson (1987: 207) reported the same kind of peer pressure: "To go out with a boy from a state [public] school was enough to make you a social outcast."

As Bob Connell and his colleagues (1982: 151) found in their 1980s research on Australian schools and social divisions, one role of ruling-class schools is to construct networks of friendship, kinship, and acquaintance within that class. This pattern is exemplified in Sydney by annual gatherings of private schoolgirls to watch boys' rowing regattas on the Hawkesbury River, or boys' athletics carnivals and football games at the Sydney Sports Ground or local private schools. These traditions were well established by the 1950s, and seemingly absorbed through osmosis or through heterosexual hegemony, as I would now call it. When Kambala girls reached what adults then called the "boyfriends" stage at around age 15, we were expected to develop a sudden interest in (private school) boys' sport as a site of courtship rituals. The female dress code at these displays of adolescent male muscle and testosterone was explicit: summer clothes and white shoes for the regatta, winter clothes and dark shoes for athletics and football, regardless of the weather. Shaving one's legs and wearing nylon stockings, despite the extreme heat of Australian summers, were among the other rigid features of the dress code.

Another adolescent courtship ritual took place on Friday evenings at Miss Cay's Dancing School, where mostly private school boys and girls, aged about 15, received instruction in ballroom dancing. The same dance teachers conducted after-school classes at Kambala from 1945 to 1959, but these were for girls only and the dress was the school uniform; hence they lacked the cachet of the mixed after-school classes. In my case, after having persuaded my father to allow me to go to the Friday classes, I managed to say something that angered him so much that he withdrew his permission. I had the option of attending the next year with girls a year younger than I was, but I avoided this humiliating experience and instead asked a boyfriend (whom I had met at the beach, not at the regatta) to teach me.

In her analysis of 1950s Australian girlhood, *The Modern Girl*, Lesley Johnson (1993: 78–79) cited a *Sydney Morning Herald* story from 1953 that exemplified how secondary school education served as "an affirmation of a normative definition of femininity." The article described how 15-year-old girls from a public "home science" high school (that is, B-stream students in the terminology of the day) had presented a "mannequin parade" (fashion show) to teachers and students. Wearing "pretty dresses, high heel shoes and lipstick—instead of the baggy tunic," the girls received accolades for their dressmaking skills.

Somewhat surprisingly for Kambala, girls from the dressmaking classes (the B stream) began staging annual fashion shows in 1956. Sounding somewhat like a breathless radio announcer, Miss Hawthorne devoted an entire paragraph in her book to the 1958 event, listing "long and short pyjamas, nightgowns, petticoats and half-slips ... blouses and skirts as worn by the younger miss ... suits and dresses in princess, chemise, sheath and empire lines" (Hawthorne, 1972: 214). Finally, she enthused,

> The garment that won the greatest admiration was worn by the Senior Prefect, Margot Thatcher. Designed and made by her, the long evening dress fitted superbly her tall, graceful figure. (Hawthorne, 1972: 215)

Like Johnson's example, this event validated femininity through both the girls' mastery of sewing and their ability to package themselves as heterosexual adult females, and the fact that the star of the show embodied "leadership" as well as "femininity" would not have been lost on Miss Hawthorne. At the same time, her public validation of students in the B stream was unusual—and it was equally unusual for the senior prefect to come from their ranks. Although there were long-standing traditions, including the annual prize-giving ceremony, concerts, and all varieties of interschool sporting competition, to recognize academic, musical, dramatic, and athletic achievements, public venues for celebrating artistic or dressmaking talents were rare in the Kambala of the 1950s.

## In Case the Queen Should Call

On the issue of social values, private schools of the 1950s were loyal to the British model in their overt as well as their hidden curriculum. Nobbs asserted that Miss Hawthorne and her predominantly Australian-born staff "instilled a sense of pride in Australian achievement, rather than fostering undue attachment to Britain and the Royal Family" (Nobbs, 1987: 114). However, Miss Hawthorne's own account made much of Queen Elizabeth II's coronation in 1953 and the Royal visit of 1954. She gave a detailed report of the boarders' enjoyment of listening to the coronation on the radio, as well as an account of students' participation in the Queen's visit. Hundreds of Kambala girls joined 110,000 other schoolchildren at the Sydney Showground (in full school uniform, of course) to watch a small figure in the far distance waving from a car.

We had extensive practice in curtseying and memorizing protocol, in preparation for the unlikely event that the Queen should stop to talk to one of us. "Your Majesty," we would say when we first responded, and "Ma'am" thereafter. A smaller group of uniformed Kambala girls also gathered on a Rose Bay street on a Sunday afternoon to watch the Queen on her way to the Bondi surf life-saving carnival. I was then able to boast that I had seen her three times, since mother had taken me—this time, wearing my best dress—to College Street where one of her lawn bowling friends lived. Ironically, I knew that some of my peers considered this inner-city section of the Queen's route to be a working-class neighbourhood, and would probably have been critical of the fact that my mother's friend lived in such a "slum" part of town.

## Gender and Careers

Some historians have challenged contemporary feminists' assumptions that gendered (that is, masculinized) language, most notably the universalizing male pronoun, has constrained the aspirations of countless generations of girls and young women. I agree, for the most part, with feminist critics who argue that some girls refused to accept "the explicit or implicit masculinity of the images of educational achievement" and were able to envision and identify with a "genderless human being" (Johnson, 1993: 9; see also Conway, 1990; Gill, 1995; Steedman, 1982). It seems that the girls who questioned or rejected masculine hegemony possessed the imagination and drive needed to transcend narrow masculinized notions of what it meant to have agency and autonomy.

Judith Gill observed the following in relation to Catholic schoolgirls of the 1950s:

> In terms of their academic curriculum the situation was ungendered—these schoolgirls had no awareness of their being precluded from understanding and identification with literary or historical heroes because they were girls ... [They] took up as their own Hamlet's procrastinations and Lady MacBeth's hand wringing, they fought with Nelson and Bismarck and Queen Elizabeth I. They begged with Oliver Twist and loved Estella along with Pip—and none said they shouldn't or couldn't because of their sex. (Gill, 1995: 3)

## KAMBALA: LEARNING TO WIN, LEARNING TO LOSE

In my case, however, holding on to a genderless image became more difficult as I matured. When I was in sixth class, Miss Epstein, apparently seeing no contradictions, asked us to use Rudyard Kipling's poem "If" with its well-known refrain "You'll be a man, my son" as a template for writing our own poems. I struggled unsuccessfully with the male pronouns and masculine symbolism until I realized that we were meant to suspend—or perhaps suppress—our female identities for the purpose of the exercise.

The universal male pronoun is jarring to contemporary eyes. The June 23, 1954, edition of the popular *Australian Women's Weekly* ("Over 750,000 Copies Sold Every Week") had a particularly striking example. Kay Melaun, writer of an advice column for girls entitled "Here's Your Answer," announced, "Everyone has *his* own answer to the burning question: How old should a girl be before she is allowed [to] have dates?" (Melaun, 1954: 35; emphasis added). She went on to offer *her* advice to a 14-year-old whose father did not allow her to associate with boys. I was a keen reader of this magazine, mainly to find horse pictures for my scrapbook; at age 11 I would not have been interested in Melaun's advice column.

By the time I was 15, I could no longer envision the "genderless human" and, in an essay on my aspirations to be a pilot, I started with the premise, "If I were a man ..." In a second leap, I enthused about the joys of flying, despite the fact that I had never been in a plane: "I think there is nothing more inviting than to be sitting aloft in the cockpit, oblivious of the world below." I wrote this during my "flying phase" when I consumed dozens of books about British pilots in World War II. My earlier "phases" and corresponding career aspirations had included nurse, teacher, jockey, veterinary surgeon, industrial chemist, and pathologist—an interesting progression into male-dominated fields after a gender-stereotypical start.

Like most schools of that era, there was no guidance department, and a short interview with Miss Hawthorne in the final term constituted "career counselling." She distributed registration forms for Sydney University and two teachers' colleges, and I ended up following a traditional feminized path by going to the Sydney Kindergarten Training College. Until I understood that I was a likely candidate for a Commonwealth Scholarship (covering university or teachers' college tuition), my parents and I had assumed that I would simply find a job after I graduated. Observing that more girls were staying in school after the minimum leaving age of 15 than had been the pattern before World War II, Miss Hawthorne noted that "in the Independent [private] Schools more did so as their parents were financially able to keep them there. But for many girls, nursing, kindergarten teaching and secretarial work in various fields absorbed those who needed to earn a living" (Hawthorne, 1972: 152).

In fact, earning a living after my three-year teacher training diploma program fitted my own goal of achieving independence very well. Kambala provided little information about university education, and, with my limited knowledge, it sounded like a continuation of school, but without the uniforms. At that stage, I didn't find this an attractive prospect, and, in hindsight, having started an undergraduate degree at age 29, I believe that university would have been wasted on me when I was only 18. With a few exceptions, all of my peers who matriculated went on to university to complete undergraduate degrees in the arts, sciences, pharmacy, or physiotherapy, and a small number did graduate degrees.

## Gender and Sex, Boys and Girls

Returning to the topic of "genderlessness," I was on firmer ground by age 16 when a teacher assigned an essay on "The advantages and disadvantages of coeducation." Public as well as private schools in

# KAMBALA: LEARNING TO WIN, LEARNING TO LOSE

Australia were still single-sex in this period, and so coeducation was seen as a novelty. This time, I did not have to pretend to be a boy. Sounding unnervingly mature, I wrote:

> When girls and boys spend their early years in the same school, a friendship grows up between the two which is different and more favourable than the so-called crushes which a teenager has ... In schools, teenagers act normally, in public they often act stupidly. If boys saw their girlfriends in school, they would form an entirely different opinion of their character and ability. In the same way, girls would admire their boyfriends much more if they went to school with them ... sitting in the same classroom, learning the same lessons, sharing the same excitement of sport or work, and growing up in each other's company.

A different kind of sexual identity dilemma presented itself when, at about age 12, I developed a crush on a girl in my class. In my creative and sexually innocent fantasy life, I pretended that she was really a boy disguised as a girl. My subsequent crush on a teacher did not lend itself to this kind of pretence. Years later, I thought that if I was attracted to a woman, it was an indication that *she* must be a lesbian, and in the case of both earlier crushes, I was correct. Some 30 years after, I sorted all this out. About 40 years later, I visited this teacher and her partner. Nell was then in her 90s, in failing health and showing signs of memory loss. Here are excerpts from my notes:[2]

> Jo greeted me at the door. Nell walked into the room using a walking stick ... She and Jo have lived in [a Sydney suburb] for 21 years. They met somewhere on the south coast. They both loved horse-riding and both taught [the same subject]. "Jo was a very congenial person," and they had a lot in common. They

got jobs in Sydney, Nell at Kambala and Jo at [another girls' school] ...

I showed Nell the picture of Liz and me ... I told her I met Liz three years ago and that we were going to buy a house and live together next year. She said, "I hope you'll be very happy, as Jo and I are."

Nell asked me twice how I had come to want to visit her again. I told her she was a very important teacher in my school days and that I admired her. I was stuck for words, especially the second time. I said I remembered her and thought of her often because she had been important to me. She said she was very honoured ...

It was a memorable afternoon, and on the ferry back to Circular Quay, I replayed the feeling of connection that my coming out as a lesbian to Nell and Jo had generated. A year or so later, I heard from a lesbian acquaintance that Nell's relatives had decided she should be moved to a nursing home some distance away from their home, and that Jo, by then in poor health herself, was able to visit only once a week when a friend drove her. To me, this seemed a heartbreaking finale to a partnership of about five decades.

Nell had been my class teacher when I was about 14, and in that role had supervised the weekly library period. After I had exhausted Mary Grant Bruce's *Billabong* series, I had difficulty finding interesting books. One day, Nell recommended what I would now call an age-appropriate romantic novel of the heterosexual variety. When she asked later whether I had enjoyed it, I responded with a firm "No." Her next recommendations were *The Hill* by Horace Vachell and *The Pea Pickers* by Eve Langley. Vachell's early 1900s novel focused on the close friendships between boys at Harrow, a private boys' school in England, and the loss one boy experienced when his best friend was killed in the Boer War.

Langley's 1942 autobiographical novel, set in rural Victoria in the 1920s, had as its main characters Steve and Blue, two young women who dressed as men and took jobs as itinerant farm workers. In 1956, an American lesbian scholar, Jeannette Foster, wrote *Sex Variant Women in Literature*, a title that clearly applied to Steve and Blue. I later discovered that both books appeared on lists of early 20th-century publications that had a gay and/or lesbian sensibility, although, being in Kambala's library, the message was largely "between the lines." I duly reported to Nell that I had enjoyed both books, especially Vachell's, and, as I recall, she was pleased.

Despite the rigid rules on gender-appropriate behaviour in Australian society, it was routine in the 1950s for private schoolgirls to play men's roles in dramatic performances, and for their male counterparts to dress up as girls and women when they put on shows. For example, Scots College, a private boys' school in the eastern suburbs, staged Gilbert and Sullivan operettas each year, with family and friends (including significant numbers of Kambala girls) applauding prepubescent boys taking the female soprano parts, and older boys in the alto roles. Such a spectacle would not be tolerated in later decades when crossing of gender boundaries became associated with homosexuality, and the practice now is for private school boys and girls to present joint concerts.

## Religion and Ritual

Ritual marked the daily lives of most school students in this era: secular and patriotic in public schools, and religious, with an occasional patriotic exercise, in private schools. Recalling his boyhood experiences in a Melbourne public school in the late 1940s, historian John Ritchie (1988: 84) wrote:

> Each week began with marching, drums and assembly, where we chorused: "I love my god and my country; I honour the flag; I will serve the King, and cheerfully obey my parents, teachers and the law."

At Kambala, we memorized all three verses of "God Save the Queen" at a young age, but it was only on the occasion of Australia's Jubilee celebrations in 1951 that we recited "I honour my god, I serve my King, and I salute my flag."

Kambala, like Frensham, Abbotsleigh, and other private schools, was founded on Christian (Anglican) principles, with daily morning prayers, weekly visits from an Anglican minister, and end-of-term church services. In a more secular vein, the singing of the school song graced most formal occasions. Incorporating Kambala's Latin motto *esto sol testis* ("let the sun be your witness"), the school song began—inappropriately, in our view—with the affirmation "Oh school we love/today with joy we're singing."

As a church school, Kambala had morning assembly conducted by Miss Hawthorne on four days of the week: a hymn from the Book of Common Prayer, the Lord's Prayer, and announcements. The minister of St. Michael's Church of England, first Canon H. Powys and later Dr. Howard Guinness, visited one morning per week for a longer service, and gave scripture lessons to senior classes (from which Jewish girls were *not* excused). About 500 girls crowded into the assembly hall—about the size of a basketball court—every morning and remained standing for up to 30 minutes during these routines.

From 1940 on, end-of-term services, with communion, were held at St. Michael's three times a year. Lined up in pairs, about 500 girls would stream out the front gate and up the hill to the church, leaving behind about 20 Jewish girls supervised by Miss Hilda Epstein. These girls, and a few others whose families came from

Europe or Asia, constituted the only ethnic minorities at Kambala at that time.

## A Woman's Place (According to the Scripture)

The 1950s generation of Kambala girls were exposed to relatively progressive educational policies and practices that emphasized academic achievement, school completion, and post-secondary education (at least for the A stream). In contrast, the conservative messages about a "woman's place," which emanated from Sydney's uniquely low Anglican Church establishment in general, and from Dr. Guinness in particular, were at odds with the school's high aspirations for most of its graduates.

On the issue of equality in marriage, Guinness had the answer: a ship must have a captain, he said, and that captain, of course, is the man. Conveniently, American evangelist Billy Graham's 1959 Australian "crusade" further entrenched that particular brand of (low church) Anglicanism. So-called marriage preparation classes at St. Andrew's Cathedral as late as 1965 perpetuated sexist views. The man, we were told, is the head, and serves as the couple's interface to the outside world. The woman's realm lies inside the house. She cooks and cleans, he takes out the garbage. This was almost as ludicrous as the notion that women should clean the inside of windows and men the outside, but the advice was delivered with a straight face to all the assembled young couples.

At a time when many working women were expected to resign when they married, Kambala followed a different path by employing several married women. Some had children, and some had been teaching for 20 or 30 years. Their presence symbolized a clear challenge to the Anglican Church's conservative view of the proper place of a wife and mother. This is not to suggest that the school was a hotbed of future women's liberationists. A lone voice at Kambala advocating women's rights was Miss Freda Skinner, senior history teacher for more than 30 years. "Don't let your husbands tell you who to vote for," she would instruct us, "and remember that women died for your right to vote!" One can only imagine how Kambala might have transformed generations of girls if teachers such as Freda Skinner had been the rule rather than the exception.

Historian Marjorie Theobald (1996: 94) identified what she termed "a discreet coterie feminism" that operated in private girls' schools from the 1880s until the 1970s. At the turn of the century, for a small number of young women from privileged families who were "intellectually ambitious," private schooling led to university graduation and, in some instances, leadership positions in girls' private schools. This kind of middle-class feminism did not undermine the appeal of private education for traditional parents who demanded "the demarcation of a female elite," and several decades passed before they began to value their daughters' future careers, and not merely their daughters' social status.

## The School Day: Learning Time, Space, and Place

Like many schools then and now, the Kambala school day was organized by bells. Lessons were 40 minutes long, and an electric bell rang in the main school building, followed by a hand bell in the junior school, to mark the ends of periods, recess, and lunch. At 8:45 a.m., a bell signalled the beginning of the day and permission to enter the classroom. Ten minutes later, another bell rang, and girls were expected to line up in assigned areas of the playground in class groups, in single file and ascending order of height, with the class captain in front and vice captain behind, ready to march into the

## KAMBALA: LEARNING TO WIN, LEARNING TO LOSE

assembly hall for morning prayers and announcements. Prefects supervised this process, which was to be conducted in absolute silence. Lateness and talking in line were punishable, and while some of my peers tell me they still have bad dreams about exams, my own nightmares often feature my late arrival at assembly.

On the first day of the school year, having marched back to our classrooms after assembly, we responded to roll call, copied down the timetable and list of required textbooks, and voted for the class captain and vice captain. Then the real work began. At Kambala, as it was at Jill Ker Conway's school, and no doubt at most schools of the era, the first order of the day was mental arithmetic, with the teacher quickly posing 10 or so arithmetic problems, and girls writing the answers. We then exchanged books with the girl beside us (to discourage cheating), the teacher read out the correct answers, we tallied one another's marks, and reported them aloud to the teacher. This public process of "taking the marks," repeated several times over the course of the day following tests in other subjects, constituted a highly visible system of academic ranking wherein we came to know our place in the competition. Jill Ker Conway was mystified by this concept of competition: her parents had always expected her to excel, but the tasks back home on the sheep station had a practical purpose, whereas at school, competition was presented as an end in itself. Even interhouse competition, discussed later in this chapter, lacked meaning for many students whose sporting and academic performance didn't produce merit points for their house.

By adolescence, we had developed a system of subverting Kambala's competitive ethos, most notably in the case of Latin, which was taught by Miss Hawthorne. Fearing her wrath and anticipating our own humiliation if we made "stupid" mistakes, we routinely compared Latin homework before school, while keeping a watchful eye for approaching teachers. Having absorbed the educational system's message that cooperation is *cheating* (Spender, 1980), I would usually correct some, but not all, of the errors I had made.

Our informal system of collaborating on homework also promoted friendships—an important function in a system where teachers emphasized individual achievement and rarely assigned group projects. (Miss Epstein was a notable exception in sixth-class English, where groups of us did improvisations of epic poems such as "Lochinvar"). Outside of house league sporting teams, the main venue for making friends was the playground, where, for all my childhood years, cliques were the order of the day. Since teachers closely supervised the lunch areas and playground, they were probably aware of these dynamics, but the girls who were marginalized, even ostracized, by the "popular" group had little or no support from teachers. Admittedly, the social components of education were not as widely recognized in the 1950s as they would be in later decades, but this hardly excuses the behaviour of one kindergarten teacher who prohibited all talking among the five- and six-year-old girls during lunch. As one of my peers recalls, she would brandish a pair of scissors to discourage "talkative" tongues.

Knowing one's place—literally and symbolically—was reinforced from a young age at Kambala. Inside the school buildings, rules included standing when a teacher entered the classroom, sitting when she gave permission, and not "crossing" a teacher on the staircase. The school grounds had clear boundaries, with the junior school having its own playground, mostly grassy and sandy areas under trees. Senior students were limited to extensive areas of concrete. The famous expanse of green lawn in front of Tivoli, overlooking Sydney Harbour, was out of bounds to all girls except prefects and officers, and, on occasion, fifth-year senior school students. It is unclear which headmistress instituted this rule, but it was strictly enforced during Miss Hawthorne's regime—if a ball

## KAMBALA: LEARNING TO WIN, LEARNING TO LOSE

strayed onto the lawn, we would have to ask a teacher's permission to retrieve it. Ironically, in 1967, the Parents' and Friends' Association created the Hawthorne Garden, a landscaped area situated right in the middle of the sacred lawn and no longer off limits to students.

The beginning of the school year, in Sydney's subtropical February heat, typically saw hundreds of Kambala girls sweltering in woollen tunics, long-sleeved blouses, and ties. After a carefree two months of bare feet and beaches, the black Oxford shoes and tight collars symbolized the school's rigid expectations. The uniform comprised grey tunics, long-sleeved white blouses, ties, grey woollen sweaters, cream Panama summer hats, grey velour winter hats, and grey bloomers. (In a major departure from tradition, Miss Hawthorne introduced a short-sleeved blouse in 1956.) Tunics could not be too long or too short; when one knelt, the hem should just touch the ground. *Every* item of clothing, including bloomers (later evolving into ordinary grey cotton underwear) had to be "regulation Kambala uniform"—that is, available only at certain department stores at inflated prices. All items were checked annually by teachers to ensure uniformity. Contemporary Canadian students' practice of "accessorizing" private school uniforms with non-regulation jackets, shoes, and jewelry was unheard of. However, the grey sweaters that my mother knitted managed to escape censure, perhaps because Miss Hawthorne didn't want to criticize her handiwork.

Any resemblance to military precision in appearance was probably intentional. At one point, Miss Hawthorne personally inspected every girl's hat to ensure that her mother had sewn on the hatband correctly, with folds of prescribed dimensions and a flat area in the middle. (The military have a more effective method, with manuals illustrating the precise coordinates for positioning badges and nametags). Hairstyles prompted further rules and regulations. No hair was allowed below the collar, unless it was tied with a grey ribbon—a rule that persists to this day. Miss Hawthorne's severest rebukes, in my recollection, were prompted by "rule-breaking" hairstyles and imperfectly removed lipstick. Deliberately leaving on traces of lipstick from the previous night was a way of advertising to peers that one had a busy social calendar, including dates with boys during the week.

On the issues of hair and tunic length, the required image was practical. Lacking a specific sport uniform in the 1950s, we played sports and performed physical culture and folk dancing in our heavy tunics. On rare occasions in extreme heat, the younger girls were permitted to remove their tunics and do indoor physical activity or school work in their blouses and bloomers. Given these constraints, manageable hairstyles and tunics of appropriate length (not too long) were sensible. The shapeless grey tunic tended to conceal the female maturation process, with breasts and hips flattened under its unflattering lines. Although, in her uniform, the ideal Kambala girl was asexual, at the same time the school played an important role in socializing generations of girls into heterosexual womanhood.

## Learning to Compete: Winners and Losers

Dedication, combined with inflexibility on the part of the headmistress, had individual and collective consequences for students, particularly on the issue of maintaining Kambala's reputation as a school that produced excellent examination results. External public examinations—the Intermediate and Leaving Certificates—had been introduced in NSW in 1912, with detailed results reported in the Sydney newspaper; in later years, the names of Commonwealth Scholarship recipients and the top 100 students in the state were also published. Every year, anxious parents would wait outside the city newspaper office to read their children's results as soon as the papers came off the press.

In the early decades of the century, there was relatively little academic pressure at Kambala and the other elite girls' schools, and little expectation that students would pursue professional careers or enter public life. Rather, the emphasis was on social graces and accomplishments. But as Noeline Kyle cautions in relation to girls' private education up to 1920,

> [t]he influence of individual, independent women in implementing a new demanding curriculum should not be overlooked in the rush to damn the refined nature of the "ladies' school" which permeated these schools still. (Kyle, 1986: 124)

The climate changed in the 1920s when only the larger and better equipped private schools could compete with the growing numbers of publicly funded high schools, and after Miss Hawthorne took over Kambala in 1933, she introduced policies and programs geared toward academic success as measured by external exam results.

In this era, middle- and ruling-class parents increasingly came to value their daughters' as well as their sons' education, largely because of the social capital that education produced. Competition between girls' private schools increased and academic excellence became a marketable commodity. It served a school's interest to be able to state in its prospectus that all Leaving Certificate (LC) candidates had passed, and that a significant percentage had matriculated (gained university entrance), achieved honours (higher level passes), and received scholarships. Indeed, as Kambala students in the 1950s, we witnessed the not-so-hidden streaming process that ensured optimal LC results. With enrolment exceeding 500 girls, Miss Hawthorne, in consultation with teachers, divided the first three years of senior school—called first, second, and third years in the NSW system—into A and B streams. (These would now be called academic and non-academic streams.)

Latin, French, and Mathematics I and II were offered exclusively to A-stream students, while those in the B stream had general mathematics, art, and dressmaking. Both streams also had English, biology, history, and geography as LC credit subjects. Sport and scripture were non-credit subjects, but there were internal exams in scripture. Throughout this era, Miss Hawthorne was adamantly opposed to introducing physics and chemistry, which, she claimed, girls did not need. Before the curriculum changes introduced through the Wyndham Report in the 1960s, the small number of Kambala girls who wished to pursue science or medicine at university had to study with private tutors outside of school in order to meet the entry requirements.

Most students in the B stream left school at age 15 after completing third year and the Intermediate Certificate, and only a very small number of these girls were permitted to proceed to the LC. The late 1950s marked the introduction of a terminal fourth year at Kambala, a change that kept students in the B stream in school until they were 16, but at the same time ensured that these purportedly low-achieving students would not bring down the level of LC results. This innovation also generated another year of fees. Miss Hawthorne would probably have experienced pressure from the School Council on financial matters, but it is clear, too, that she devoted considerable energy to maintaining Kambala's academic reputation.

Having thoroughly absorbed Kambala's achievement ethos, I decided to drop history and geography—subjects for which I had only gained Bs—at the end of third year, when it was necessary to select six out of the eight subjects that I had taken up to that time. My program was now English, French (honours), Latin, mathematics I and II, and biology, and I was pleased to discover that there was now no room in my timetable for sport and physical education. Responding to my choices, Miss Hawthorne warned me that a person who does not know history is not "properly educated." In 1983, having studied history and sociology at the graduate level, I wrote to tell her that I was now fully educated, and reminded her of her earlier advice!

It was widely rumoured among my peers that it was futile for parents to ask Miss Hawthorne to let their daughter move from the B to the A stream, or continue to fourth and fifth years if she had decided otherwise. At age 15 or 16, many graduates of the B stream headed for a year at Miss Hale's Secretarial College, a short career in office work, and early marriage. Despite its purported superior education, Kambala's retention rates in the 1950s were similar to those in the public system, where more than half of the female students had left school by age 15. Only 4.7 percent of public school girls were still in school at age 17, compared to 8 percent of boys (Johnson, 1993: 77).

In the 1950s and 1960s, however, early school-leavers without training could readily find employment. The concept of "school dropout" had no currency, and, according to Judith Gill, no stigma (Gill, 1995), but this did not mean that there were no negative consequences for young women. Labour force figures for the 1960s showed that 80.7 percent of employed women had no training, compared to 67.6 percent of males, with women representing the least educated group in the workforce, as well as having the lowest status and pay (Dixson, 1976: 39).

Girls assigned to the B stream were not "dumb"; rather, they failed to thrive in Kambala classrooms, where authoritarian teaching practices and the iron hand of the headmistress favoured girls who were highly motivated and competitive, while appearing to obey teachers and rules. Many former students of the B stream completed university as mature students, and others enjoyed successful careers in business without post-secondary qualifications, thereby demonstrating that Miss Hawthorne's streaming decisions were sometimes off the mark.

Penny Nelson wrote about her memories of academic competition during her years at Kambala:

> From second class onwards, as hundreds of girls sat nervously on the floor, Fifi used to read aloud the competitive marks of every child in the school, every half term. The few who got results in the eighties or nineties would be congratulated. When she reached fifty and below she would add comments such as "Carolyn Angstrom, absent with appendicitis, forty-eight; Vivienne Adams, forty-six, no excuse." I still remember this ritual as one of the most horrible I've had to endure. Perhaps out of fright, I managed to get marks in the sixties or seventies despite being away a lot, with colds and childhood diseases, but especially with asthma. (Nelson, 1995: 37–38)

Her words evoke memories of the anxious flutter that passed through the ranks as Miss Hawthorne issued the command for the youngest class to sit, thereby signalling a long assembly and the inevitable reading of marks. For some, this was an exercise in public humiliation that took place six times a year with the reading of half-term and end-of-term marks. Along the same "public shaming" lines, classroom teachers read out and posted the results of mid-year and end-of-year exams, which were introduced in fourth class. Although absolute silence was expected during assembly, I do not recall any intervention on Miss Hawthorne's part when her announcement of failing grades or multiple detentions prompted shocked and disapproving gasps from the more self-righteous girls.

Not all private girls' schools embraced competition to the extent that Kambala and Miss Hawthorne did. At another Anglican school, Abbotsleigh, in the 1950s, the philosophy of education was to "think, work, play, and live" (Burrows, 1968: 93), while Ascham, a non-denominational girls' school, adopted the "Dalton Plan" of monthly assignments and study periods—both more holistic approaches than Kambala's. When Penny Nelson left Kambala after fifth class and became a boarder at Frensham, in Mittagong, NSW, she found a school with "half as many girls ... ten times as much space" and a completely different institutional climate:

> The school felt free and friendly. No lining up. No saluting the flag. No glove inspections. Amazingly, no marks! In theory, the school favoured cooperation, not competition. Workbooks were marked with As, Bs and Cs, and personal comments, but never with numbers. (Nelson, 1995: 74)

## "Doing One's Duty": The House System

The house system at Kambala, as in other Australian schools, was modelled on the long-standing practice in British boarding schools, ostensibly to generate "team spirit" through academic as well as sporting achievement, and to foster a sense of belonging within the large and impersonal school population. However, I found that Kambala's house system did more to entrench competition, conformity, and a militaristic hierarchy than to promote a sense of community.

Each girl was assigned to a house—Roseby, Wentworth, or Gurney—when she began her schooling. House captains, prefects, and officers, totalling more than 30 girls, were elected by the senior classes, under the supervision of the teacher who served as house mistress and the headmistress. Full house meetings were held each term. I recall that, at age seven, my announcement that I had to attend a "meeting" the next day was met with considerable mirth by my father. The only meetings that my parents ever attended were those of their respective lawn bowling clubs, held once a year.

As Miss Hawthorne (1972: 109) explained the house system, "each house was on duty for a week in rotation and the captain and officers were responsible for organizing their girls to carry out duties connected with grounds, sports equipment, sweeping, etc." The duty system generated routines and responsibilities that would have been onerous for many seven-year-olds: checking the house notice board on Monday morning to see which cleaning duty was assigned, presenting oneself to the prefect at the appropriate time and place, and, under her supervision, completing the task quickly to allow some playtime before the bell rang.

Although Kambala girls were not expected to litter, the lunch and playground areas always yielded food scraps and papers to be picked up. Sweeping floors and picking up litter may have seemed inappropriate for daughters of the ruling class, but the duty system persisted for decades, perhaps because it reinforced traditional notions of the female role—specifically, the idea that cleaning up other people's messes was useful preparation for the roles of wife and mother. These kinds of cleaning duties were not, however, assigned to private school boys.

In Miss Hawthorne's words, the house system provided all girls with "the opportunity of proving and developing their sense of responsibility and their reliability" (Hawthorne, 1972: 109). In practice, Kambala's prefect system rewarded those with "leadership" qualities, defined as good behaviour, reasonable academic and sporting achievement, and self-confidence, by giving them responsibility for policing their peers. The most blatant example was "gate duty," wherein a prefect scrutinized every girl exiting the school to ensure that she was wearing full school uniform: tie, hat, gloves, and blazer in winter. Offenders' names were listed and repeat offenders were disciplined. As Jill Ker Conway (1990: 101) recalled, private school uniforms, emulating the British model, were totally impractical for hot Australian summers, but socialization as a "lady" required girls to value propriety over comfort. At Kambala, this brand of "propriety" included superhuman bladder control during school trips, since there were some occasions when we were forbidden to use public toilets.

Vigilance over uniforms extended outside the school grounds, where anonymous adult eyes, whom we assumed to be oversocialized Kambala old girls, could be relied upon to report to Miss Hawthorne any instances of an incomplete school uniform or inappropriate behaviour that signified failure to live up to our "superior" social standing. In third year of senior school, when our class decided to have a post-exam celebration at a local milk bar, where we mingled with Catholic schoolboys, phone calls came in fast and furious. The next day, after the predictable fierce admonishments in assembly, Miss Hawthorne announced two new school rules: outside of the school grounds, no Kambala girl shall eat while in school uniform, and no girl shall talk to a boy while in school uniform.

The duty system may have appeared to serve as a kind of a social leveller in the junior years, with every girl taking her turn at keeping the school tidy, but it also entrenched the privileged status of prefects vis-à-vis the rank-and-file, thereby conveying an important lesson in meritocracy. Prefects were also implicated in Kambala's punishment system by setting and supervising detentions. Once a week, Miss Hawthorne read out the names of girls whom teachers had disciplined for "bad" behaviour. These girls received "order marks" and after-school detentions as the result of two order marks in one week, or, worse still, "Saturday mornings"—a punishment for repeat offenders who had to serve their detention in school uniform on a Saturday.

In her reflections on prefects, a well-known private school old girl who later became Sydney University's Chancellor, Leonie Kramer, recalled an incident from her school days, also in the 1950s, at Melbourne's Presbyterian Ladies' College. She explained how she had confronted "a couple of girls, prefects, who were frightful snobs. They were fiddling around with the duty roster and I got stuck into them. I had a burning sense of injustice" (Kramer, cited in McGregor, 2001: 270). She credited the school with providing "strong training in moral obligations and responsibilities," but it seemed that the two prefects were untouched by this training.

## More Winners and Losers: Sporting Competition

As Miss Hawthorne explained in her report for 1940, "Sport was compulsory for every child, all secondary classes having three, and the primary four classes per week which included drill [physical culture], tennis, netball, folk dancing and games" (Hawthorne, 1972: 109). From 1920 to 1931, she had been a sports teacher at St. Gabriel's girls' school, one of the last to be operated by Anglican nuns, where she and her friend Hilda Epstein had been both pupils as well as teachers. Jill Ker Conway's headmistress, too, had promoted physical activity and sport at Abbotsleigh, and had herself been a successful amateur athlete, and both heads had completed classical university degrees.

Miss Hawthorne clearly valued sporting competition and regularly publicized and praised individual and team successes in her Monday morning announcements of winners, losers, and scores attained in interschool meets. Year after year, detailed results of the annual (private) girls' interschool swimming and athletics carnivals appear in Miss Hawthorne's inimitable handwriting on the

KAMBALA: LEARNING TO WIN, LEARNING TO LOSE

programs stored in Kambala's archives. She could have assigned this task to a sport mistress, but apparently chose to do it herself because of her interest in the events. In addition, the annual reports that comprise much of her book provide full details of interschool sporting competition results.

In 1934, Miss Hawthorne reported that the Association of Headmistresses of NSW (a group of private girls' school principals) had "unanimously agreed that too much publicity was being given to schoolgirls' sport which was not in the best interests of the game or the girl." They resolved to have a trial year with no cups or trophies, and no points awarded in tennis, basketball (netball), and field hockey. Furthermore, interschool tennis and basketball matches were to be reduced by half and "played on a geographical basis to reduce the strain of travelling" (Hawthorne, 1972: 119). These concerns appear to have surfaced somewhat later than in other Western countries and were short-lived. In contrast, in the United States and, to a lesser degree, in Canada, the campaign aimed at eliminating sporting competition for girls and women was well underway by the late 1920s and persisted until the 1940s (Lenskyj, 1986).

Interestingly, the diluted level of competitive sport had some unanticipated consequences, and in 1950 Miss Hawthorne noted disapprovingly that Kambala's basketball teams and tennis teams did not *lose* any of the four matches played against other schools in the eastern suburbs region. She went on to explain:

> We asked if we could have more matches (they were played on a geographical basis) and against some larger schools the following year so that the danger of too much success might be minimized by some defeats. (Hawthorne, 1972: 174)

In the interests of promoting a sense of fair play, she believed, with some justification, that a good athlete should learn how to lose as well as how to win. The limited competitive opportunities available at this time often resulted in unbalanced teams and unsatisfying matches.

Miss Hawthorne's attention to physical activity might suggest that athletic achievement was valued as highly as academic results at Kambala. The most "successful" girls, however, combined excellent academic achievement, impeccable conduct, leadership qualities, and a reasonable level of sporting ability. A record of poor marks or conduct was not completely wiped clean by athletic achievement, even when it brought honour to the school, but athletic achievement enhanced a reputation already established in the academic realm.

Kambala girls of the 1950s received contradictory messages about the importance of sporting achievement. On the one hand, innate talent was rewarded and successful athletes were recognized for their efforts and for the credit they brought to the school. In some instances, these girls' parents had recognized their daughters' abilities at an early age, and had arranged private coaching or membership in a community track and field club. On the other hand, girls who lacked athletic ability, had no outside coaching, or did not play games with siblings and friends outside of school were unlikely to improve their performance. The elements of throwing, catching, and hitting a ball were poorly taught, and there was no instruction in running or swimming. A lap around the oval, about 400 metres, constituted the start of the sport period for older students, but it was routine, or perhaps fashionable, for most girls to slow down to a walk at the halfway point and to collapse at the end.

Typical of the era, teachers routinely chose girls to be captains for team sports (proceeding alphabetically through the class list), and these girls in turn picked teams based on athletic ability and popularity. Failing on both scores, I was always the last on the bench, with the only relief from this humiliation occurring when it was my own turn, or my best friend's turn, to be captain.

School swimming in the summer months comprised a weekly leisure swim (supervised but with no instruction) at Watson's Bay baths, a harbourside pool that was barely swimmable at low tide. Girls who were "indisposed" (menstruating) were excused from swimming but required to accompany the group to Watson's Bay. An indoor pool was constructed at Kambala in the 1970s, somewhat later than in other private schools in Sydney, and the annual school swimming carnival was for many years held at the Olympic pool at Milson's Point. Interschool swimming meets among girls' private schools in Sydney were first held in 1916 at the Drummoyne Baths, and later moved to the Domain Baths. Then, for the next six decades or more, the Olympic pool was the venue.

In another example of long-standing "private school tradition," girls' interschool athletic competitions, first held in 1921, became a fixture at the Sydney Sports Ground from 1926 on (Hawthorne, 1972: 62). For reasons never made explicit, Kambala girls did not participate in hurdles competition until 1960, even though it had been included in the girls' interschool athletic carnival for decades. Rumour had it that Kambala sports teachers, or perhaps Miss Hawthorne herself, harboured traditional fears about the injurious effects to female virginity of "doing the splits."

## Conclusion

Like some of Gill's participants, I'm left with a range of feelings about Kambala: On the one hand, gratitude that my parents valued education, appreciation for the few competent and caring teachers, and pleasure in the lifelong friendships made at the school. On the other hand, I feel profound disappointment with a curriculum and school climate that aimed at reproducing ruling-class values, narrow religious beliefs, and an individualistic world view. I do not credit the school with promoting critical thought, understanding of social justice, or consciousness of oppressions, but perhaps it is unrealistic to expect 1950s teachers to have valued these educational goals. As Australian journalist Fiona Capp (2004) noted in her review of the private-school genre of films, novels, and memoirs, while the schools prided themselves on their successes, personal stories often focused on their failure "to value individuals who do not measure up to conventional notions of success or proper behaviour." However, like Laura, the hero of the well-known novel and film *The Getting of Wisdom*, I discovered as an adult that my apparent "unfitness" in the narrow world of Kambala proved to be "another aspect of a peculiar and special fitness in that freer, more spacious world."

PART II

INTRODUCTION TO PART II

# Toronto, Canada:
# Two Feminist Awakenings

Lesley Johnson identified two genres of feminist autobiography or "feminist awakening" stories: firstly, Betty Friedan-type accounts of women's self-realization as human beings, and secondly, Carol Gilligan-type accounts of women's self-validation as having *different* voices and identities to men's. Johnson (1993: 20) concluded that both genres should be seen as "specific political strategies devised at particular points in history" to generate political and public identities for women. The next part of the book, in which I discuss my participation in parent activism and feminist/lesbian politics in the university, provides personal examples of these strategies at work.

As I noted in the introduction to Part I, Sue Middleton's work has influenced my approach, and I found that the categories generated by her life history interviews closely matched the ones that I had already developed: family, sexuality, career, formal education, and feminism/politicization (Middleton, 1993: 73). This is not too surprising, given that I have been immersed in women's studies since 1979. However, I clearly recall a time in 1970 as a suburban wife and mother when my world view was very different. I had started reading a library copy of a book by one of the early feminists, probably Betty Friedan's *Feminist Mystique*, and it didn't take long until I realized that this was dangerous knowledge. I knew that if I continued reading there would be no turning back—I wouldn't be able to ignore my raised consciousness and simply go about the business of being a wife and a mother. So I returned the book to the library unread, and consciously postponed my feminist education for almost 10 years. Even in 1978, a year made memorable by an experience of sexual harassment and failure to gain tenure at Townsville College of Advanced Education (Australia), I was reluctant to attribute any of these experiences to gender. In the interim, however, I completed my undergraduate degree (avoiding women's studies!) and gained valuable leadership experience in a school-community organization, as the next chapter will demonstrate. This was a stage in my life when self-realization as a political human being—Friedan's concept of feminist awakening—was central.

The year 1979 marked the occasion when I literally became "a card-carrying feminist" by joining the Feminist Party of Canada, and I started a graduate program in women's studies at the Ontario Institute for Studies in Education the same year. For the next 25 years, self-validation, as Gilligan defined it, developed in the context of lesbian-feminist politics.

In her 1996 book, *Parent-School Collaboration*, American feminist sociologist Mary Henry defined a feminist approach as a "collaborative, socially concerned way of thinking," rather than the mechanistic, bureaucratic model characterized by competitiveness and individualism.

> Central to the discussion of a feminist view of organizational structures and school leadership are the notions of (a) an ethic of care and connectedness; (b) collaboration and community building; and (c) a focus on the core technology of teaching and learning. (Henry, 1996: 19)

Henry defined technology as "the means or methods of accom-

## INTRODUCTION TO PART II

plishing the goals of education" and went on to identify systemic problems in education arising from White male privilege and the marginalizing of women and ethnic minorities (and, I would add, sexual minorities). These are recurring themes in the next three chapters, where I examine the struggles of Toronto parents, particularly mothers, to have a voice in educational decision making, followed by an analysis of developments in women's studies and feminist pedagogy in the university.[3]

CHAPTER 4

# Activism, Education, and Mothers

In this chapter, I'll begin by bridging the gap between the subject of Part I—the 17-year-old girl who has just completed the Leaving Certificate at Kambala—and the 28-year-old woman, now married and the mother of two young children, one just starting junior kindergarten at Frankland Public School, Toronto.

I trained for three years as a preschool and primary school teacher at the Sydney Kindergarten Training College, taught in two private schools in Sydney, then married and moved to Toronto in 1966. After living in downtown and suburban apartments for several years, our family moved to a house in the east end of Toronto in 1971. The next year I started my undergraduate degree in sociology at the University of Toronto, as well as working part-time in English as a Second Language programs for parents and preschool children. At that stage, I had no experience in community organizing. When I lived in the suburbs, my notion of activism was to put up notices in the apartment laundry room urging residents to use environmentally friendly detergents. I was soon to discover a whole new world of community politics in downtown Toronto.

## Citizen Participation: The Radical 1960s

Sherry Arnstein's "Ladder of Citizen Participation," first published in 1969 and still widely cited, became the standard by which radical community groups in Toronto, like their counterparts elsewhere in Canada and the United States, evaluated their involvement in decision making at City Council and the Board of Education. Like many of my contemporaries, I found her work invaluable in exposing the hidden agenda of top-down initiatives in a variety of community and school contexts. Genuine citizen participation, Arnstein argued, required the following:

> the redistribution of power that enables the have-not citizens ... to be deliberately included ...[and to] join in determining how information is shared, goals and policies are set, tax resources are allocated, programs are operated ... it is the means by which they can induce significant social reform which enables them to share in the benefits of the affluent society. (Arnstein, 1969: 216)

Starting with the bottom rung of the citizen participation ladder, manipulation, Arnstein observed, "In the name of citizen participation, people are placed on rubberstamp advisory committees ... for the express purpose of educating them or engineering their support" (Arnstein, 1969: 218). Similarly, therapy, in the guise of citizen participation, seeks to "cure" victimized groups of their "pathology" rather than eliminating the causes of their victimization: poverty, racism, and other forms of systemic discrimination. In the 1960s and 1970s Ontario educational context, as the following discussion will show, "Opportunity Classes" and "parent education" constituted the schools' therapeutic services of choice for low-achieving children from low-income families and their parents.

## ACTIVISM, EDUCATION, AND MOTHERS

The third level, informing, is a one-way, top-down channel of communication in which those in power simply seek community endorsement. Consultation and placation are techniques wherein citizens' (free) advice is sought by policy makers, primarily to send out a positive public relations image. In the decades since Arnstein developed these concepts, the power of the public relations industry and its spin doctors to shape the public image of government bureaucracies has arguably exceeded 1960s activists' worst predictions.

On the positive side, partnership, delegated power, and citizen control constitute the top three levels of Arnstein's ladder. As radical community organizers of the 1960s expressed it, the goal was not to make the poor more comfortable in the ghetto, but to eliminate the ghetto. Chicago-based community organizer Saul Alinsky spoke of helping the "have-nots" to gain a "piece of the bourgeois pie." Clearly, an equitable education system was a key factor in achieving these goals, or at least in enabling the next generation to enjoy enhanced socio-economic security.

Eventually, those in power began to recognize the rights and capabilities of citizens to share in making decisions that affected their lives across a range of areas, including urban planning, public housing, education, health care, and legal services. The community school movement, like other examples of citizen participation and community activism, began in North America in the 1960s in protest against the generally paternalistic, bureaucratic decision-making processes in public education. Specifically, parents identified the class bias that manifested itself in middle-class teachers' low expectations of working-class children, children of immigrants, and children who were Black or Native. In short, as one group of low-income Toronto mothers asserted, "Downtown kids aren't dumb" (Park School Community Council, 1971). And they might have added, "Downtown mothers aren't dumb, either!"

In 1972, a Toronto parent group called the Community School Workshop identified the following aims of the "community control" movement in education:

1. the improvement of our education system through a process of decentralization of decision-making
2. the creation of a system in which all elements of the school community (students, teachers and adults) take part in determining and engaging in the educational process
3. the use of the community as a total learning environment
4. through the above, to develop better understanding among parents, students and teachers. (cited in Martell, 1971: 76)

## Toronto Mothers Fight Back

In Toronto, the widespread tendency for school administrators and city bureaucrats to treat "parents" or "residents" as an undifferentiated mass of gullible, incompetent individuals had prompted serious grassroots opposition by the late 1960s (Keating, 1975, 1979; Martell, 1970; Repo, 1977). The actions of a group of low-income mothers living in Trefann Court are generally credited with breaking new ground in parent organizing. Trefann Court was an inner-city neighbourhood served by Park and Regent Park elementary schools, Castle Frank High School, and Eastdale (girls') and Parkway (boys') vocational schools. (At that time, *all* of Toronto's special education high schools and vocational schools were situated south of Bloor Street, in an area with a high proportion of working-class and immigrant families). The Regent Park public housing project, north of Trefann Court, was home to about 5,000 adults and 5,000 children in the early 1970s.

In 1969, the Trefann Court Mothers decided to put forward a

candidate, Noreen Gaudette, for the school board elections. Frustrated by a year of fruitless meetings with teachers and board officials, they prepared a brief protesting the Opportunity Class (special/remedial education) system, which, they concluded, was "little more than a babysitting service" (Martell, 1970: 33). Some teachers with whom they had discussed the problem didn't hesitate to compare Park School—unfavourably—to the "good" schools in middle-class neighbourhoods like North Toronto. But, as one mother observed, "We'd be darn fools to move to a better district and live in one room just so our kids could go to a good school. We shouldn't have to" (quoted in Lorimer, 1969: 7). The Trefann Court Mothers' brief embodied their frustration and pain as they documented how Opportunity Classes and teachers were meaningless and irrelevant to their children:

> [It] doesn't touch the world as it's experienced by people who don't have much money, who are forced to take society's hard and boring jobs, who are constantly threatened by welfare officials or the police ... So the kids slide away ... To put this another way, it appears as if the school system directly discriminates against children from poor families ... (cited in Martell, 1970: 29–30)

The brief reported that "graduates" of two-year programs in high schools such as Parkway and Eastdale usually ended up unemployed or in unskilled, dead-end jobs, despite the purported vocational training that such schools offered.

In a radical and creative community initiative in the fall of 1969, these mothers established their own alternative, Laneway Community School, with the help of the Varsity Downtown Education Project, a University of Toronto student initiative. By its third year, it had two full-time certified teachers and nine students aged nine to nineteen years. The emphasis was on basic skills, especially reading. A board of parents and teachers set school policies, and parents were required to attend all meetings. Initially it had operated along free and unstructured lines, but at the end of the first year, parents, teachers, and students unanimously agreed that a structured setting was essential (Laneway Community School, 1972).

Except for Laneway's success, there were few changes in downtown schools, and in 1971, many of the same mothers, along with other Park parents and teachers, established Park School Community Council for the purpose of examining academic issues, most notably the poor school performance of downtown children. The council's efforts also helped the school to obtain a grant from the Donner (charitable) Foundation to hire local parents as paid teacher aides (Education in Downtown Toronto, 1972).

In November 1971, Park School Community Council prepared a brief entitled "Downtown Kids Aren't Dumb: They Need a Better Program," which members presented to the Toronto Board of Education. At an earlier meeting of the board's Fundamental Skills Committee, three men—a school trustee, a superintendent, and a teachers' federation representative—had all publicly expressed the view that children from low-income downtown families had lower "innate ability" than middle-class children. The parents and teachers who wrote the brief rightly accused the superintendent of allowing their children "to be disgracefully slandered" (Park School Community Council, 1971: 9). They went on forcefully to assert that

> it is not our kids who are at fault but the society they have to grow up in ... [There is] a great iceberg of prejudice in our schools ... [M]uch of it comes from the mouths of those who tell us they've come to help us ... to help keep poor kids, working class kids, at the bottom of society, where their parents have been. (Park School Community Council, 1971: 10–11)

Gender as well as social class issues in the educational context of the 1960s and 1970s are important. In the gendered hierarchy of the elementary school system (junior kindergarten to grade 6), teachers were predominantly women, with a few exceptions in the higher grades, while most vice principals, principals, and superintendents were male. Of the parents who became involved in schools, either as volunteers in the classroom or as members of parent-teacher groups, most were women and, in low-income neighbourhoods, many of these women were sole-support mothers. Among Toronto trustees, a small number were women, including progressives such as Fiona Nelson, but men were in the majority. These demographics were reflected in an image that often appeared in the mainstream media, as well as in community-based publications such as *This Magazine Is about Schools*: a downtown mother vehemently expressing her views to an impassive group of middle-aged White men in suits.

## Home and School Association, or Community Council?

Until the 1970s, Home and School (H&S) associations remained the traditional way in which school boards channelled and controlled parental interest without encroaching upon the "professional" territory of the teacher. As Kari Dehli et al. (1988) argue, community groups that organized on education issues in the late 1960s and early 1970s correctly perceived H&S groups as part of the education "establishment." They were either "neutral" or pro-board, and their existence sometimes hindered efforts to organize an independent parents' organization (Dehli and Januario, 1994; Dehli et al., 1988). In 1973, the president of the Toronto Council of Home and School Associations was quoted in the *Toronto Star* (April 25) as saying:

> We're not interested in running the schools. I don't think parents are equipped to make judgments about financing and staff. In the area of curriculum, we would like to give our suggestions and a lot of parents would like to work in the school as volunteers, but the actual methodology—that should be up to the professionals.

And, as late as 1974, Ward 7 trustee Doug Barr, one of the more progressive voices on the board, asserted that "most [educators] seem to have realized that few parents in Ward 7 want 'control' of the schools but they do want accountability, easy access and in some schools, active participation and partnership."

Prior to 1971, Frankland's H&S Association had operated on traditional lines, with mothers organizing bake sales and hosting afternoon teas. According to the minutes of meetings between 1964 and 1971, the group's activities generally fell into two categories: fundraising for student awards and equipment, and "parent education" seminars presented by Board of Education officials or other "experts." The February 1968 minutes clearly demonstrated how the group provided the principal with a forum for top-down parent education. On the issue of a new student assessment scheme, according to the minutes,

> [the principal] proceeded to give an explanation of, and his personal views on the Continuous Progress Plan, as opposed to the traditional Graded School Plan ... [and] invited those present to question him on the *merits* of the Continuous Progress Plan. (emphasis added)

A summary of conference resolutions presented in the Ontario *Home and School Bulletin* in May 1973 demonstrated key concerns at that time: control of vandalism, school bus safety regulations, retail sales tax, nursing assistance in schools, weighting factors in school budget ceilings, moral values in the *Schools Act*, testing for colour blindness, evaluation of junior kindergartens, community use of schools, and television violence. While these were important issues, they were "safe" insofar as they didn't encroach on the professional domain of principals and teachers.

## Riverdale Gets Organized

By the 1970s, Toronto's east end neighbourhood of Riverdale, the area in which Frankland Public School was located, was also becoming a hotbed of community activism. In 1969, Riverdale had the distinction of mounting the first mass-based community organizing project in Canada, when a group called the East Don Urban Alliance (later called the Riverdale Community Organization—RCO) hired a community organizer to tackle local issues ranging from public transit and pollution to urban renewal and public housing. Don Keating, the organizer, had trained and worked in Chicago with Tom Gaudette, "the dean of community organizers in Chicago," whose approach drew on Saul Alinsky's work (Keating, 1975: i). At an early RCO meeting that I attended, I was surprised and somewhat shocked when Keating called for an adjournment, and proceeded to lead us to a demonstration outside the home of a "slum landlord" on a nearby street, in a typical Alinsky-style direct action. Instead of staying with the protesters, I returned home, disappointed that the "real" meeting hadn't taken place. November 1972 marked the occasion of Canada's first community convention, at which RCO was renamed the Greater Riverdale Organization. I attended the convention as one of several delegates representing Frankland Community Council, the parent-teacher group formed in 1972.

City and school officials, however, were slow to credit Riverdale residents with even a small amount of political savvy. It appeared that many of those in positions of power characterized the neighbourhood as "ethnic"—Greek, Italian, and Chinese—and mostly working class. Even one of Frankland's more progressive teachers publicly referred to the area east of the school as "full of tacky insulbrick houses"—in front of parents who lived in these modest woodframe houses that were typical of the Riverdale neighbourhood.

In the early 1970s, Withrow Area Residents' Association (WARA), of which I was a member, expressed concern at the low level of maintenance, particularly litter cleanup, in Withrow Park, just down the hill from Frankland School. One resident, during a deputation to City Council, graphically demonstrated the problem by dumping a bag of broken glass that he had collected in the park onto the floor of the council chambers. A few months later, emboldened by WARA's confrontational style, I wrote a letter of complaint to the parks commissioner about the negligent supervision and dirty water in the park's wading pool, went to his City Hall office, and refused to leave until I could hand it to him personally. By this time, city bureaucrats should have realized that residents' groups such as WARA were a force to be reckoned with. But, a few months later, in response to our request for the upgrading of the children's playground, the Department of Parks and Recreation sent officials to make a presentation to WARA. The two men unrolled a blueprint of the new design, and proceeded to ask residents whether we would prefer the playground entrance to be located on the southern or eastern end. Needless to say, we refused to be placated by this blatant tokenism.

## Time for Change: Parent Involvement

In 1968, the Ontario government released the findings of the Hall-Dennis Committee, which had examined the curriculum and program in publicly funded elementary schools. The report, *Living and Learning*, presented several recommendations in the areas of "community liaison" and "parental involvement." These included courses for parents on child development, parent committees in every school district, and the recruitment of parent and community volunteers, as well as resource people with specific skills, to help with in-school and out-of-school activities.

Frankland Public School led the way on many of these issues. Around 1970, a kindergarten teacher had started a volunteer parent program. By June 1971, several others teachers had shown interest in following her example, but many had not. In a related initiative, parents and teachers had been discussing plans for a new parent-teacher council that would, among other tasks, implement the volunteer program by recruiting "liaison parents" for each participating teacher. But, as the minutes of the H&S meeting on May 31, 1971 revealed, teachers had mixed responses:

> The obvious resistance of some teachers to the proposed council was commented on and accepted. Teachers are professionals and some do not appreciate having parents in the classroom in a liaison role. They prefer to work with individual parents.

At a public meeting in September 1971, the proposed new model was presented and names of prospective parent volunteers were collected. By November, nine teachers were participating and nine mothers had agreed to be "liaison parents" and to coordinate and recruit other volunteers. Given my teaching background and my interest as a mother of two young children, I offered to serve as liaison parent for my daughter's kindergarten class. Although initially very reluctant to take on this kind of responsibility, I soon discovered that I enjoyed it, so I volunteered in the kindergarten two half-days a week as well as filling the liaison parent role.

Although teachers and parents consistently used the gender-neutral word "parent" at the time, it was primarily the middle-class mothers who volunteered in the classroom; most fathers and many working-class mothers were at work during the day. Although about 60 percent of students were Greek, about 80 percent of the liaison mothers and classroom volunteers were Anglo-Saxon. Among the mostly middle-class parents who chaired various school-community committees in the 1970s, several were part-time or full-time teachers in other schools or educational programs, while many of the fathers who served on the building committee for the new school were engineers or architects. There was usually gender balance as well as some ethnic diversity among the parents on these committees, but they remained predominantly middle class. Women were in the majority as teachers, with the exception of a few men teaching grades 4 to 6, and the principal and vice principal were male. Middle-class Anglo-Saxon parents and teachers were over-represented in leadership roles, but this should not diminish their dedication and commitment. As Dehli and Januario (1994: 6) observed, these women and men "spent hundreds of hours, and innumerable evenings and weekends in pursuit of a better, more relevant, democratic and just school system."

At a January 1972 meeting, parents and teachers renamed the former H&S group the Frankland Community Council (FCC), and the offices of chairman (*sic*), secretary, and treasurer were filled; I agreed to serve as secretary. By this time, I was an enthusiastic parent activist—perhaps too keen, in the view of some teachers.

Monthly meetings of parents and teachers were held to discuss the volunteer program as well as other issues, and the tone was generally optimistic. However, in individual conversations with parents, I sensed some frustration that was not surfacing in FCC meetings, probably because of their reluctance to voice any criticism in front of their children's teachers. Trying to elicit liaison parents' real responses, I circulated a letter describing some of my own mixed reactions to the liaison parent program and inviting comments. I suggested that, despite some parent participation and the new mandate of FCC, parents were still not actively involved in any significant decision making in the school. Responses confirmed that liaison parents, most of whom had long histories with Frankland's former H&S, were resigned to the fact that teachers and administrators would never extend real decision-making power to parents. One mother refused to reply in writing, and later told me that she wanted to avoid the entire issue because she didn't want to jeopardize what she saw as the "good relationship" that she had with her child's teacher. Like many of the mothers, she found that the dual roles of parent and FCC member presented difficulties. "Teachers have us over a barrel," parents would often say to me. Despite the rhetoric about teachers' "professionalism," many parents feared that their outspokenness on school board issues might have negative repercussions on their own children's classroom experience.

I compiled the responses to my letter and used them as a basis for the agenda of the May 17 FCC meeting. Some exploration of issues such as volunteer training and teacher-parent relationships ensued, but other topics proved too uncomfortable for open discussion, especially the question, "Can parents approach the [teaching] staff on a basis of equality or is there a social and cultural gap between them?" My final questions were asked rhetorically (since we all knew the answers):

> Are parents given the opportunity to discuss curriculum, discipline, traditional and progressive methods of teaching, achievement tests, sex education, etc., with the staff? Would such discussion bring about changes if it were mutually agreed that changes were necessary?

There was, in fact, an unspoken rule that, behind the closed door of the classroom, "teacher knows best." Mothers were used/useful in adjunct roles: assisting individual children, going on field trips, and instructing in the after-school program. Fathers were used/useful when a new school building was in the works. Curriculum was an area designated "No parents allowed." In other words, teachers and principals determined how parents should be deployed; these were not joint school-community decisions.

In this age of electronic communication, it may seem outdated to mention the importance of the printed word. However, as a parent with good writing skills (thanks to Kambala), good typing skills (thanks to evening courses in 1970), and an old manual typewriter, I was able to produce FCC newsletters, parent questionnaires, minutes of meetings, and other print materials that changed the power dynamics between parents and teachers. It was usually the principal and teachers, rather than parents, who controlled the content and distribution of these kinds of materials, but as FCC gained power, this pattern changed.

The volunteer program started again in September 1972, but for various reasons many liaison parents did not continue in that role. For those teachers with a well-established group of volunteers, coordination by a liaison parent was no longer needed, and some teachers preferred to do this task themselves. I compiled a list of volunteers in June and distributed it to all teachers in September. Seven teachers and about 30 volunteers were now involved. The following September, three additional teachers invited parent volunteers, but the number of those helping on a regular basis dropped to about 20. A total of about 30 volunteered in classrooms, after-school programs, school trips, and FCC committees.

In October 1973, teachers learned that the board was planning budget cuts that would reduce the number of teaching assistants at Frankland from five (one per kindergarten, and one primary) to three, to be shared by the four kindergartens. Some of the teachers embarked on a course of action to fight this proposed cut, but failed to involve FCC parents. Although at first this initiative involved only teachers, the name "Frankland Community Council" appeared on two letters that they sent to inner-city schools and to the Toronto Board of Education. In response, as FCC co-chair, I called an emergency FCC meeting to discuss these actions, to voice objections to the process, and to set in place a procedure for future emergency decision making. It appeared that some teachers had phoned individual parents to explain their own position on the issue, and to urge them to attend the next board meeting in a show of solidarity. There was no opportunity for FCC to have a full public discussion of the issue so that the parents could decide for themselves whether or not they agreed with the strategy. At worst, this incident resembled Arnstein's manipulation rung on the citizen participation ladder, and, at best, the placation rung. In short, parents were not treated as full partners in political strategizing and decision making. For pragmatic reasons, however, those present at the FCC emergency meeting endorsed the letter after the fact.

By 1974, 13 Toronto public elementary schools had been designated as "community schools." About one-third of the schools had parent volunteers working in classrooms and after-school programs, accompanying children on field trips, or working at home on school-related tasks. Thirty schools had after-school recreational programs, with varying proportions of voluntary and paid instructors. In middle-class areas, these programs had between 75 and 100 percent volunteer staff, whereas in downtown working-class schools, the volunteer component was usually under 50 percent, and short-term government grants were sometimes used to pay instructors.

## Knowing One's Place: Parents and Teachers

The boundaries between parents and teachers were complex. Realistically, it was not surprising to witness the "them/us" split, but the FCC parents who were middle class and Anglo-Saxon themselves were reluctant to admit that a power differential existed between the two groups. I cannot imagine any FCC parent, even cynically, echoing one Trefann Court mother's assessment of teachers: "They know everything, they've got everything under control, and we're just a bunch of *** (*sic*) idiots" (quoted in Lorimer, 1969: 7).

Social class differences were played out on a bigger stage at one community meeting organized by the Toronto Board of Education in a middle-class neighbourhood when several parents speaking from the floor began by introducing themselves as working-class people. Some middle-class parents then came to the microphone and announced, sarcastically, that they too "worked for a living," thereby undermining any notion of parent solidarity in the face of board bureaucrats who were engaged in a superficial attempt at community consultation.

Some of the FCC mothers, and a few fathers, occupied a middle ground as a kind of "honorary teacher" who felt relatively free to enter the staff room, to use the office copying equipment, or to talk to the principal or vice principal without scheduling an appointment. I sometimes had this ambiguous status when I was FCC chair or co-chair, coordinator of Frankland's after-school program, and supply teacher. Inappropriately, in my view, the principal sometimes shared with me his prejudiced views of some female teachers.

My status, however, had clear limits. I recall one winter day when I was in the school office struggling to operate the antiquated Gestetner copy machine, and succeeding only in sending sheets of paper flying over the office floor. Of the several staff members who walked past carrying cups of coffee, no one offered me either help or coffee. On a more serious note, I bore the brunt of some teachers' undisguised resentment when I made interventions on behalf of my own children. One teacher, for example, accused me of acting as if my children should get special treatment just because of my FCC role. I found this disconcerting since I believed every parent was entitled to make the kinds of requests that I did on behalf of my children, although only a minority did so at that time.

## Greek Parents Start Organizing

The year 1974 saw a repeat of citizen placation at the Board of Education level, this time on the issue of a proposed Greek cultural program at Frankland. The board convened a "technical planning work group" to develop and present a draft program at a public meeting when community response would finally be invited. When FCC objected to the schedule, we were told that this was "a curriculum matter" that must be left to the "experts." *Globe and Mail* reporter Loren Lind documented the board's co-optation of this initiative in his 1974 book, *The Learning Machine*. As he explained, the board had rejected Greek and Italian parents' requests for actual language instruction (termed "third language instruction," after English and French) within school hours the year before. Greek parents, this time mostly fathers from Frankland and Jackman schools, had expressed serious concerns about their children's inability to communicate with them in Greek. The official response was to permit students to have a 30-minute "cultural program," not a language program, staffed by volunteers, at no cost to the board (Lind, 1974: Chapter 2).

FCC as a group supported the Greek parents' initiatives and, in broader terms, respected their stated preference for holding separate FCC meetings conducted in Greek, in addition to attending regular FCC meetings. However, some individual Anglo-Saxon parents—at that time a minority at Frankland—had mixed responses to the proposed Greek language program. One Frankland mother who responded to the principal selection questionnaire (discussed below) expressed the view that the new principal should "work to *keep* the school Canadian" (emphasis in original) and went on to ask, "Why should one group expect our school to cater to their background? ... If they [Greeks] want to keep their old customs they should open separate schools ..." In fact, a well-attended private "Greek school" that taught the Greek language was operating at Frankland every day around the dinner hour, and parents were rightly concerned that their children missed the family meal in order to learn Greek after school.

## Curriculum Councils

In another top-down curriculum development in 1974, the Toronto Board of Education voted to establish what it called a "curriculum council" in each of the six school areas of the city for the stated purpose of increasing "communication concerning the schools within our communities." The letter distributed to parents in Area Four, the east end area of Toronto where Frankland was located, stated that a steering committee of teachers, parents, principals, and students "under the direction of the Area Superintendents" had met to plan the council's activities, and was circulating the attached questionnaire in order to determine areas of interest.

Actual interest in any aspect of the proposed council was low. Although 17,000 students in 28 schools were given notices for their parents, only 113 parent responses were received, representing an average of 4 per school, along with 18 teacher responses.

The chief concerns identified by both parents and teachers were English as a Second Language, parent-teacher communication, and school-community relations. Mathematics and discipline were additional areas of concern noted by a small number of parents. One collegiate principal claimed, perhaps with good reason, that the 6 "negative" parent responses from his school indicated "a complete lack of interest, serious lack of understanding or a combination of both."

One elementary school mother's comments confirmed that the information given to parents was inadequate: "I am especially interested in a council being formed," she wrote, "so if a parent wants help for her child she could discuss it with the council." Other parents were equally confused about the purpose of the council. Some offered suggestions based on traditional views of education and gender: more homework; dress codes; harsher discipline; real learning, not "play" in kindergarten; spelling and penmanship; training in "manners" and respect for the law and the police; sewing and cooking for girls, and manual training for boys. A small number of parents and teachers mentioned educational problems stemming from the low socio-economic status of many families.

Minutes of curriculum council meetings from May 1974 to June 1975 reflected the steady entrenchment of a top-down approach. A stream of "experts"—teachers, principals, consultants, librarians—gave presentations on curriculum topics, while parents, myself included, were occasionally asked to speak on non-curriculum issues, including parent volunteer programs, reporting to parents, and producing a parent-teacher handbook. Of the average attendance of 30 per meeting, 20 were educators and 10 were parents (Area Four Curriculum Council, 1975: Minutes, April 16), with a fairly balanced gender representation. (When I looked at the record of those present at these meetings, I recognized the name of a teacher, Ken Zeller, whose tragic death, discussed in the next chapter, prompted the Toronto Board of Education finally to address the pervasive problem of homophobia in the schools.)

Further east, the Area Five Curriculum Council was even more rigidly organized. The area superintendent served as "chairman," a secretary-treasurer was appointed, and the council "membership" and attendance at meetings was limited to 12 parents and 12 teachers. Organizers of this area's curriculum council, it seemed, did not even pretend to aim at inclusiveness, and only one meeting—on the topic of discipline—was open to the general public, that is, to *all* parents and teachers.

On the broader issue of discipline, the use of the strap or any other form of corporal punishment had been abolished by the Toronto Board of Education in 1971 after the second attempt on the part of progressive trustees to eliminate these forms of punishment. Records showed that the strap had been used 760 times in the 1969–1970 school year, and 196 times in 1970–1971. Speaking against abolishing the strap, Ronald Jones, the Toronto Board of Education's director of education at the time, urged trustees to use "education" rather than legislation to eliminate strapping. Representatives of the elementary Toronto Teachers' Federation and the Toronto Public School Principals' Association both spoke against its abolition, and progressive trustee Gordon Cressy, somewhat surprisingly, tried unsuccessfully to have the corporal punishment issue put in the hands of local school-community councils (Lind, 1971). Yet, as late as 1974, there were parents who advocated a return to corporal punishment. In the opinion of one Frankland parent, "Teachers and principals should be very strict ... Strap should be brought back, to put fear into the students who think going to the office [as punishment] is fun." Those opposed to the strap prevailed and the issue was not revisited.

## Stepping over the Line: Principal Selection

In 1973, following the news that the current principal was due to retire in June 1975, FCC began to discuss ways of democratizing the board's principal selection process. After months of intense organizing and lobbying, a parent and a teacher from Frankland were eventually permitted to sit on the board's principal selection committee.

A 1973 survey of Frankland's teachers showed that most were eager to have a voice in principal selection, in conjunction with the administration. The questionnaire asked teachers for their views on who should determine the criteria, screen and interview applicants, and make hiring recommendations. Many teachers were opposed to trustees' and parents' involvement, especially in the interview and recommendation stage. Overall, trustees gained lower teacher support than parents, even on the relatively non-controversial issue of determining selection criteria. This was an era when teachers and principals tended to view trustees as "the other side," partly because trustees were the elected representatives of local residents, whose priorities might conflict with teachers' interests. It was not until later in the 1970s that progressive teachers and trustees at the Toronto Board of Education formed successful political alliances.

In the 1974–1975 school year, the Toronto Board of Education began testing a new principal selection procedure. In the past, only board administrators had processed the applications of principals seeking transfers, and the only acceptable way for local communities and teachers to participate was through the submission of criteria to guide the selection committee. The new system of screening and interviewing was to be carried out by a committee comprising administrators, trustees, and Toronto Teachers' Federation representatives. It was against this backdrop that FCC made the radical proposal of including parent, teacher, and community voices on the committee that would choose a new principal for Frankland following the retirement of the incumbent.

Because the school administration had played a paternalistic role for so long, teachers and parents in some communities viewed any proposed change as a threat. For example, in October 1973, teachers at Winchester Public School indicated that they were not willing to participate in the selection of a new principal, nor did they want parents included in the principal selection committee. When this kind of direct parent and teacher involvement came up for discussion as a board-wide policy, a parent from South Parkdale Residents' Association was quoted in the *Toronto Sun* (November 1, 1973) as saying: "We are going to fight this—it's just one more move by the leftwing reformers to undermine the present school system."

Similarly, on the topic of the principal's relationship to the community, one Frankland teacher stated: "I don't think that the principal should take any 'pushing about' from parents or pressure groups in the community." A Frankland parent made a veiled reference to the Greek majority when she expressed the hope that "he will not be influenced by or in favour of any one particular ethnic group because of its majority and will give equal consideration to others."

In December 1974, FCC established a Principal Selection Committee, which convened a public meeting for January 30, 1975. The flyer that the committee sent out to parents asked the provocative question, "You pay the price ... Do you think you should choose the goods?" At this meeting, FCC passed the following motion: "The parents and staff of Frankland School be involved in the decision-making process for the selection of a new principal."

While FCC members—about 30 parents, teachers, and community people—were unanimous in their support of this change, some of the invited Toronto Board of Education guests were, predictably, "seriously concerned" about this threat to the status

## ACTIVISM, EDUCATION, AND MOTHERS

quo. Area Superintendent Helen Sissons led the naysayers by posing questions on assorted topics: a parent referendum, voting procedures, qualifications, access to "confidential" personnel files, community involvement in firing decisions, and effects on teachers' morale. Finally, she predicted that good applicants would be "deterred" by community involvement, and questioned whether FCC was really acting "in the best interests of the children." Even the usually progressive trustees were lukewarm in their support, recommending instead that FCC should follow the new system currently being tested so that it could be given a fair trial. Parents were undeterred. Countering the administrator who challenged FCC's representativeness, one father asked how well the Board of Education represented the Frankland community.

In conclusion, according to the minutes, one of FCC's co-chairpersons "emphasized that parents attending the meeting didn't view themselves as activists, but as parents concerned with the education of their children"—probably a reaction to Sissons's earlier question. In reality, many of us were proud to claim the name "activist."

Two later FCC meetings, on February 6 and 20, produced additional motions:

1. We ask that we be allowed to put two members, elected by the FCC, on the final selection committee—one of whom will be a teacher ... and one ... a parent.
2. That the FCC will undertake to formulate criteria which will be forwarded to the Board, to act as guidelines in the screening process ... and as guidelines for those FCC representatives ...

Significantly, a closed meeting of Frankland teachers on February 19 passed, by a 76 percent majority (that is, about five or six negative votes), the following motion: "We, the teachers of Frankland

Public School, agree with the principle that the FCC seek direct representation ... [on the principal selection committee]." Finally, the Representative Assembly of the Toronto Teachers' Federation supported the Frankland initiative at its March 13 meeting. On April 24, FCC selected one teacher and one parent—both men—as its representatives on the board's principal selection committee.

A questionnaire in Greek and English was distributed to all Frankland parents (estimated at 300–400 families) in order to generate criteria to guide the FCC representatives. Only 30 responses were received, and only 2 were from Greek parents. Greek parents also met with a Greek-speaking social worker from the Board of Education to discuss criteria, and from these meetings came the proposal that the new principal should understand the Greek community and should uphold strict discipline. Most questionnaire responses identified predictable qualities and attributes: the ability to establish rapport and work cooperatively with students, staff, and parents; a good record of recent primary teaching; and proven ability to generate a good working relationship with the community. Eight respondents used the male pronoun only, nine referred to he/she, and thirteen did not specify. In the summer of 1975, a non-Greek male candidate was selected for the position.

Unlike the radical Trefann Court Mothers who had set up an alternative school and hired their own teachers, FCC took the liberal/reform route of working *with* the system, and what began as a radical community initiative produced a relatively predictable outcome. At the February 6 FCC meeting, Graham Scott, a Frankland parent and former trustee, had put a $5 bill on the table and urged us simply to place an advertisement in the employment section of the *Globe and Mail*. We discussed his proposal at the February 20 meeting, but it gained limited support and no action was taken.

## The Co-optation of Parent Involvement

Despite the promising start in the 1970s, radical parent groups failed to thrive, partly because of severe cutbacks to publicly funded educational systems and partly because of the conservative political backlash of the last two decades. In many boards, a diluted and depoliticized definition of "parent involvement" has replaced the earlier emphasis on grassroots community organizing and development. In their critical review of this area of educational research, Dehli and Januario (1994: 9) concluded that it tended to have "a narrow evaluative focus" on student achievement outcomes, with only a small number of North American studies examining issues of power and inequality within parent-school relationships. For example, in his review of 45 articles on "parent involvement research" published between 1978 and 1994, John Wherry (2003) concluded:

> When schools work together with families to support learning, children tend to succeed not just in school, but throughout life. In fact the most accurate predictor of a student's achievement in school is *not income or social status*, but the extent to which that student's family is able to: create a home environment that encourages learning; express high (but not unrealistic) expectations for their children's achievement and future careers; become involved in their children's education at school and in the community. (emphasis added)

Dr. Wherry may sound like a school administrator, but in fact he was president of the Parent Institute in Virginia, USA. He went on to summarize benefits for students, including higher grades and test scores, better attendance and behaviour, fewer placements in special education, and higher graduation rates and enrolment in post-secondary education. Parents involved in schools had more confidence in the school as well as in themselves as parents; they supported the school more and gave teachers higher ratings. Teachers in schools with parent involvement had higher morale and "higher opinions of parents and higher expectations of their children," and those schools had better reputations in the community. Finally, in Wherry's assessment, "Parent involvement leads to feelings of ownership, resulting in increased support of schools and *willingness to pay taxes* to support schools" (emphasis added). To say that Wherry lacked any identification with working-class and poor parents is an understatement; in fact, his position fits near the bottom of Arnstein's ladder of citizen participation—"engineering support."

## Conclusion

The pioneering efforts of groups such as the Trefann Court Mothers, Park School Community Council, and FCC paved the way for other parent and community groups to participate in the Toronto Board of Education's decision making in a number of areas: principal selection, third language instruction, school building design, class size, specialist teachers in elementary schools, and community use of school facilities. These were exciting times—my "formative years" as an activist. Learning how to conduct a parent meeting using Roberts' Rules had been the only part of my teaching training that had slight relevance to the task, and, like many other politically active parents at this time, I learned on the job. In the 1970s and early 1980s, parents were encouraged to see that the Toronto Board of Education was making structural changes to encourage community representation on a number of its committees. However, there were limits to the board's embrace of citizen participation, as the next chapter will demonstrate.

CHAPTER 5

# More Activism: Challenging Homophobia in Toronto Schools

Despite the many obstacles, some community and parent groups in Canadian and American school districts, especially those in large urban centres, were successful in pushing boards of education toward implementing progressive policies and programs. By the late 1970s, their demands that school curricula and programs should take gender, class, and ethnic differences into account were producing some results, but issues of sexual orientations generally remained "in the closet" until the mid-1980s.

By this time, I was a relatively new lesbian-feminist activist, and a part-time instructor in women's studies at the Ontario Institute for Studies in Education (OISE), University of Toronto. I was also active in OISE's Centre for Women's Studies in Education (CWSE), and, as the CWSE representative to the Toronto Board of Education's Status of Women Committee, I helped to develop the curriculum guide on homophobia and sexual orientations.

## Sexual Orientations and Human Rights

Gay and lesbian liberation groups active in Ontario in the 1970s tended to give priority to legislative issues such as the decriminalization of homosexual practices and basic human rights protection.[4] Before these changes were enacted, there were compelling reasons for gay and lesbian teachers and students to conceal their sexual identities. And, although there were gay men and lesbians who were parents of school-age children, they were also likely to stay closeted, given court decisions denying them custody on the grounds that they were unfit parents. Hence, gay and lesbian invisibility remained a common pattern.

In the 1970s, the Toronto Board of Education created several new staff positions, including school-community relations and race relations workers, employment equity officers, and women's, labour, and Black studies coordinators. Similar developments in the board's structures resulted in community representation on several of its standing committees—Status of Women, Race Relations, Black Issues, Heritage Languages, and Human Sexuality—and, for a short time, there was a committee on gay and lesbian concerns. However, many of these initiatives suffered drastic cutbacks as a result of right-wing swings following municipal and school board elections in the early 1980s, and the entire School Community Relations Department was disbanded in 1985 (Dehli et al., 1988).

In December 1986, after years of lobbying by gay and lesbian groups, the Ontario government introduced sexual orientation into its Human Rights Code as prohibited grounds for discrimination. This new provision protected gay and lesbian students from being expelled from school, and gay and lesbian teachers from discrimination in employment. Around the same time, a small number of lesbians and gay men began to speak out publicly about the unchallenged heterosexism and homophobia in the school system, and about the harassment and violence experienced by gay and lesbian students and teachers.

A Toronto Board of Education policy in place since 1981 had prohibited discrimination in employment on the grounds of sexual orientation, and the board's 1991 sexual harassment policy also covered homophobic harassment. However, the 1981 policy had included a clause stating that the board would "not tolerate the proselytization of homosexuality." While the exact meaning of the clause was obscure, it deterred many teachers from speaking out on explicitly gay and lesbian issues for fear of being accused of "recruiting."

## Curriculum Transformation and Anti-homophobia Education

Feminist theorists, including Peggy McIntosh (1983) and others, developed a phase theory of curriculum transformation, which moves from the womanless phase to the "exceptional woman" phase, then on to "woman as problem" and "women on their own terms." Finally, an inclusive curriculum takes gender, social class, race/ethnicity, and sexual orientations into account.

There are clear parallels in the area of curriculum change that seeks to integrate lesbian and gay issues, starting with the "invisible" phase, then introducing the "famous gays" phase, then on to "clinical" portrayals of gays and lesbians, and so on. Until the 1980s, most publicly funded educational systems in Canada remained at the "invisible" phase, with a few isolated ventures into the "famous gays" phase. In 1989, when the Toronto Board of Education first attempted to introduce these topics into the curriculum, the "clinical/pathological" approach—the idea that sexual minorities are more to be pitied than blamed—was the dominant one.

Phase theory has been criticized for its linear progression, its reformist tendencies, and its portrayal of curriculum transformation in managerial rather than political terms (Collins, 1991). Most significantly, there is no clear route for the politicization of curricular decision making through involvement of, and accountability to, members of the disadvantaged groups in question. Given this flaw, it would be possible for educators to include material on the minority group, but to ignore issues of power and privilege: misogyny, racism, classism, homophobia, and the other "-isms." Similarly, in liberal educators' hands, the focus may be exclusively on the need for protection from discrimination, while the underlying (hetero)sexist, racist, and classist frameworks and content of the curriculum remain unchallenged.

Patricia Hill Collins, a Black feminist educator, proposed an analysis that began by investigating the self-defined, subjugated standpoints of subordinated groups, particularly on questions of knowledge production. Secondly, she called feminists to challenge dominant frameworks—that is, those developed by and for White, male, middle-class, heterosexual interests. Her third step was the reconstruction of knowledge and the formation of an inclusive curriculum, with previously dominant frameworks now constituting only one of many standpoints.

Applied to gay and lesbian issues, Collins's model offers several important insights. The "famous gays" phase, while addressing the problem of invisibility, is elitist, while the "clinical" approach that characterized the Toronto Board of Education's draft curriculum on sexual orientations is both offensive and dangerous. Rather, the process of giving visibility and voice to subordinated groups—in this case, gays and lesbians—demands a radical rather than a reformist approach. Events at the Toronto Board of Education demonstrated the conflict between the reformist approach of board staff and the radical approach of gay and lesbian activists. Board staff were concerned primarily with protecting gay and lesbian students and staff from harassment or unfair treatment, while avoiding being perceived as "condoning" their sexual practices, whereas the activists' goal was to present lesbianism and homosexuality as valid sexual choices, equally "normal" and "natural" as heterosexuality.

## Lesbian and Gay Teachers' Activism in Toronto

Like many aspects of gay and lesbian history, activism among gay and lesbian teachers has not been well documented and has often proved difficult to research. The following review of some Toronto-based initiatives suggests that many lesbian and gay community leaders were involved in broader political groups such as the Coalition for Lesbian and Gay Rights in Ontario (CLGRO), established in 1975, rather than in single-issue groups concerned with education.

A lesbian-feminist teachers' support group formed in Toronto in 1985, and met monthly for over a year for discussion and support. Subsequently, a second group was established and met regularly at the Woman's Common, a women-only restaurant and social club. Neither group engaged in direct political action or lobbying. In fact, the Woman's Common group was divided over this question, with some members interested in activism and others opposed to it. The Toronto Board of Education Lesbian and Gay Employees' Group was formed in the spring of 1990 and met monthly, primarily as a support group. Other lesbians and gays interested in educational issues were welcome, and I attended several meetings. As with the lesbian teachers' groups, in which I also participated, there were often debates over the balance between business (political activism) and social (mutual support) activities.

Outside of lesbian and gay groups, there was little activism by teachers' unions or associations in this area, primarily because of fear of public hostility to the idea that gays and lesbians were working with children. The (now amalgamated) Federation of Women Teachers' Associations of Ontario (FWTAO) had a resolution on its 1990 annual general meeting agenda calling for action on homophobia, but it was tabled, apparently because the member who proposed it was absent, and it did not reappear on the 1991 agenda.

Although the FWTAO raised a feminist voice on many social problems, there was, for the most part, a resounding silence around lesbian issues at this time.

In the early 1990s, there were several public forums on gay and lesbian concerns in education in Ontario. In February 1991, Tim McCaskell, a student programs worker with the Toronto Board of Education, addressed these issues at a panel sponsored by the Committee on Homophobia, a student-faculty group at the University of Toronto. In his presentation, he compared the board's progressive programs and policies on race and racism to its relative neglect of gay and lesbian issues and the pervasive problem of homophobia in the schools. McCaskell recommended curriculum initiatives, including cross-curriculum programs, links to other oppressions, and the use of lesbian and gay community resource people in the schools. More broadly, he called for institutional, system-wide changes in policies, sanctions and rewards, affirmative action programs, and staff training.

In the subsequent discussion, as in other contexts where lesbians and gay men reflected on their school experiences, a common theme emerged. For those who had discovered their gay or lesbian identities while they were high school students, even as late as the 1980s, this period in their lives was one that they remembered with profound pain. In fact, it seemed that many gays and lesbians preferred not to reflect on their adolescence at all. This pattern may have contributed to the relatively low level of community organizing around homophobia in schools at the time.

A conference on the theme "Out in the Classroom" was organized by the Coalition for Lesbian and Gay Rights in Ontario and Guelph Gay and Lesbian Equality in November 1991 at the University of Guelph. One of the first in Ontario, the conference provided an opportunity for about 100 participants to hear documentation of the education system's refusal to deal with gay and lesbian concerns, as well as some success stories about students' acceptance of "out" gay or lesbian teachers. Coming from a variety of regions and educational contexts, we were able to develop networking and lobbying strategies, and formed a working group to continue discussing strategies for change.

## Breaking New Ground: A Student Conference on Homophobia

November 1991 marked the occasion of the first conference on homophobia and sexual orientations for Toronto Board of Education students. The board had discouraged organizers from pursuing their initial goal of making this a board-wide event that would have required central administrative approval, and the delicate balance of progressive versus conservative trustees and the imminent election made it unwise to push the issue too far. Therefore, organizers decided to have a smaller conference for students from the board's five alternative high schools, and the event was publicized only through alternative school staff and principals.

Small group discussions were organized around basic issues as well as specific topics such as religion and ethnicity. In the various workshops I facilitated or attended, most students had very little knowledge or understanding of lesbian and gay sexualities, but many expressed their strong support for freedom of sexual expression and were outraged that gays and lesbians experienced discrimination. The vast majority of students really wanted basic information: What causes someone to be gay? What do gay men do? What do gay women do? Aren't you afraid of catching AIDS? Workshop leaders answered all these questions, and then attempted to direct the discussion to some commonplace heterosexist assumptions—for example, instead of focusing on what causes homosexuality, we raised the question, "What causes heterosexuality?"

Many of these adolescents were surprisingly uninhibited when they saw that, as workshop leaders, we were prepared to answer even their most outrageous questions. Although, in an ideal world, teachers who are openly lesbian or gay are more effective examples to students than workshop leaders who have no continuing relationship with them, the very absence of an ongoing relationship made it possible for both sides to be less guarded in their exchanges about explicit sexual practices. Significantly, most, if not all, workshop leaders came out as lesbian/gay to their groups, and enjoyed the open and honest discussion that ensued.

Afterwards, a parent of an alternative school student was vocal in her complaints to the board and to the media. She claimed that her daughter had been forced to attend the conference. The student had to attend because she had used up the quota of classes that she could miss without losing credit for the year. Toronto's right-wing newspaper, the *Toronto Sun,* covered the story, which was picked up by its counterparts in other provinces. However, when trustee Alex Chumak took up her cause in a motion to request "a formal report on the conference," it was defeated, and progressive trustee Olivia Chow successfully moved that a report be made on the development and implementation of a system-wide anti-homophobia curriculum.

Chumak also expressed his views on curriculum changes that addressed gay and lesbian issues: "If all these courses are taught by gay and lesbian activists, then I would be concerned. I would want to see some balance" (quoted in Visser, 1991). This purportedly liberal concern with "balance" was also evoked in the selection of the first advisory committee for the board's curriculum guide on homophobia and sexual orientations. In its ranks were two psychiatrists, Ron Langevin and Joseph Berger, whose dated views of homosexuality as pathology were clearly homophobic. (Some of Langevin's work was also criticized for its misogynist, racist, and classist content; see Angus, Kerr, and Lenskyj, 1991).

On the matter of balance, another position in discussions of educational initiatives holds that gay and lesbian sexualities should not be presented in too positive a manner, lest impressionable and vulnerable young people find them too appealing. Mere knowledge of alternatives is seen, according to this argument, as a threat to the "delicate balance." For example, the *Toronto Sun* quoted a mother who worried that homosexuality might be portrayed as too "desirable," and a Toronto psychologist who referred to adolescents being "pushed in an unhealthy direction" (Blizzard, 1990).

Overall, there was growing interest and concern on the part of the Toronto gay and lesbian communities about educational issues, and those of us who were educators, in particular, monitored the Toronto Board of Education's attempts to introduce a curriculum unit on homophobia and sexual orientations with guarded optimism.

## Background to the Curriculum on Homophobia and Sexual Orientations

In June 1985, a gay male teacher-librarian, Kenneth Zeller, was beaten to death by four male students who attended the board's high schools. This tragic event served as a catalyst for major policy and curriculum change within the board, including the production of the curriculum on homophobia and sexual orientations that is the focus of this discussion.

Early in 1986, trustee Olivia Chow, working with lesbian and gay students and organizations, began to investigate the situation in Toronto high schools. She found virtually no curriculum material on homophobia and sexual orientations in sex education programs and noted that, since board policy at that time required that the topic be discussed only by physical education teachers, human rights and tolerance aspects of the issue were ignored in the curriculum. Students told Chow that teachers often witnessed verbal or physical harassment and did nothing to intervene on behalf of gay or lesbian students (Chow, 1986).

The policy that was eventually approved by the Toronto Board of Education in April 1986 focused on curriculum and professional development. It included the following recommendations: that "discrimination, harassment and violence will not be tolerated" in school environments; that steps would be taken, in collaboration with the Ministry of Education, to develop programs to "sensitize students to the basic human rights of *all* students and staff of the Board, including those who are homosexual"; and that inservice training programs should be provided for *all* teachers, not just physical education teachers (Chow, 1986; School Programs Committee, 1986).

A further positive outcome of this policy was the 1989 appointment of a sexuality counsellor to work with lesbian and gay students and their families, as well as lesbian and gay parents. A student support group began to meet weekly throughout the school year at the Education Centre, and a support group for lesbian and gay parents was set up in 1992. Tony Gambini, the sexuality counsellor, made presentations to students upon request by school personnel. For lesbian and gay teachers, services included monthly meetings, counselling, and referrals. All teachers were offered professional development opportunities, resource materials, and consultation.

In terms of curriculum, the AIDS epidemic had a significant impact on approaches to sex education across Canada, and the Ontario Ministry of Education's mandatory AIDS curriculum opened the door for freer classroom discussions of sex in general, and sexual orientations in particular. The curriculum guidelines were quite explicit about "safe alternatives" to conventional penetrative (heterosexual) sex, including "talking, masturbation, fantasizing and close physical contact without intercourse" (Ministry of Education, Ontario, 1987: C:38). The AIDS curriculum discussion guide also provided a brief but insightful analysis of compulsory heterosexuality:

> In spite of the fact that the majority of young people are heterosexual, they have no experience of heterosexuality. They have simply assumed that they are heterosexual because that is the societal norm. Heterosexuality can represent success and acceptance by one's peers whereas homosexuality is seen negatively. (Ministry of Education, Ontario, 1987: C:39)

By 1988, the Ministry of Education curriculum guidelines for physical and health education (intermediate and senior divisions) included sexual orientation among the topics for discussion within human sexuality. However, as late as 1990, at least one public board in the province took a stand against ministry guidelines. The York Region Board of Education, an urban area just north of Toronto, issued its own guideline banning any formal lessons, debates, or class discussion of homosexuality. It required that students under 18 obtain parental permission to do independent study on homosexuality or abortion, which were characterized as "value-laden issues that virtually defy unbiased presentation" (Ross, 1990). Interestingly, York's superintendent of curriculum apparently saw no bias problem or values conflict in discussing such issues as family planning, teenage pregnancy, commercial sex, or prostitution, to name some of the other controversial topics in the 1988 ministry guideline.

# Toronto Board of Education's Curriculum: Draft 1

The Toronto Board of Education's plans to develop the curriculum on homophobia and sexual orientations for high schools included its appointment of an 11-person advisory committee. No member was openly gay or lesbian, nor was there a gay/lesbian member who was directly accountable to a community-based group. A curriculum-writing team began work on the first draft in the summer of 1989, and it was released in January 1990. Some members of the advisory committee subsequently expressed serious concerns about the lack of consultation during the writing stage.

In a misguided attempt to impress upon teachers the seriousness of the issues confronting gay and lesbian youth, the curriculum guide clung to a disease model and a clinical perspective. There was a strong emphasis on suicide, family conflict, high-risk sexual practices, promiscuity, loneliness, and alienation from parents, siblings, and friends—presumably intended to alleviate fears about unduly "attractive" portrayals of gay and lesbian "lifestyles."

Ironically, one of the most vocal reactions to the first draft came not from parents but from Toronto's gay and lesbian communities. For example, in meetings over the summer of 1990, the Lesbian and Gay Employees' Group examined the document and developed an extensive list of problems and necessary revisions, as well as new teaching ideas. The group sent a strongly worded letter to the superintendent of curriculum in October, with copies mailed to every member of the Committee on Bias in the Curriculum. I represented the Status of Women committee on that committee, which reviewed all board-produced curriculum materials for sexist, racist, homophobic, or other bias. The letter referred to the document's "clinical character" and identified "serious flaws which constitute bias, and which contribute to continuing prejudice against lesbians and gay men." Finally, it called for *accountable representation* (McCaskell and Gambini, 1990). The superintendent's reply identified some steps that would be taken "as part of the continuing consultation process": a possible meeting with the advisory committee and a copy of the revised draft (Wright, 1991).

The November 1990 meeting of the Status of Women Committee considered a letter dated October 15 that I had submitted, expressing my own and others' concerns about the curriculum document. As an academic with knowledge of the issues and as an active member of Toronto's lesbian and gay community, I was appointed as the committee's representative on the writing team to revise the curriculum in the summer of 1991.

In May 1991, the Gay Fathers' Chapter of the Gay and Lesbian Parents' Coalition, representing a consensus of 200 parents, wrote a lengthy critique of the curriculum, identifying a homophobic bias and an overall negative perspective. As they explained, "The opening paragraph in the introduction ... sets the tone for the course. 'In all known societies heterosexuality is the pattern for most people'" (Gay Fathers' Chapter, Gay and Lesbian Coalition, 1991).

The curriculum was field tested in health classes in Toronto schools from September 1990 to June 1991, after which all the teachers involved were interviewed. Overall student response to the curriculum was not encouraging. Teachers reported instances of hostility and homophobia, especially among male students whose families held traditional religious values regarding the role of women, and who, it seemed, derived their masculine identities by using women and gay men as negative reference groups. Nor were the responses of the teachers themselves particularly positive. Tellingly, the lesson plans that teachers frequently took up in the field-testing phase were those that dealt with family histories, relationships, and values—in other words, activities that they could safely conduct without referring to homophobia or to gay and lesbian issues.

## The Revision Process

The writing team that revised the curriculum met with board staff for the first time in July 1991. As specified in the contract, I agreed to take major responsibility for revising and rewriting "Part One: Information about Sexual Orientations," and for revising "Part Two: Specific Strategies for Teaching the Unit on Sexual Orientations." The other contracted writer, a male physical and health education teacher, also revised Part Two. Board staff emphasized that I must adopt a "middle-of-the-road" rather than a "gay activist" approach, and that my work must reflect a "scientific base of research" and be "fully substantiated." It was clear from this discussion that staff were sensitive to right-wing backlash over what they perceived as a groundbreaking initiative. Several references were made to irate phone calls from right-wing parents, but it appeared that progressive parents rarely called the curriculum office.

At the end of August, largely as a result of my request, the writing team met with Tim McCaskell, the student-programs worker. Tony Gambini, the sexuality counsellor, was also invited, but was out of town. The group discussed the teaching ideas at length, and I distributed draft copies of my new Part One, which incorporated the concerns of the Gay Fathers' Group and the Employees' Group, as conveyed to me through written reports and meetings and consultations I had had with individuals and groups over the summer.

I received very little feedback or communication about the progress of the second draft between August 1991 and February 1992, except for the assurance that my material was being used with the possible exception of "two or three sentences." I (wrongly) assumed that I would receive a copy of the second draft before it was sent to the printer. At the February Status of Women meeting, I raised the issue of lack of communication, and a motion was passed to investigate the status of the document. I then found out that the second draft was already at the printers, and I received a copy the last week of February. My new work had been "cut and pasted," and the sequence and flow had been destroyed. Most significantly, another person's work had been "pasted" into the middle of my chapter in a way that undermined my intent, contradicted my conclusions, and introduced new, unsubstantiated ideas and glaring inaccuracies. The problem was not just a personal one for me; it was a political issue for the lesbian and gay communities to whom I was accountable. As I asked rhetorically in a memo dated March 9, 1992, "Would a white staff person presume to edit and editorialize on an analysis of racism developed by a Black curriculum writer who represented a Black community?"

The Status of Women Committee subsequently established a subcommittee to investigate the issue, and sent a letter to the director of education asking for an explanation of the process. Members of this subcommittee engaged in an unusually forthright discussion of the political process, even to the point of discussing whether we would insist that the entire document should be withdrawn, and a new process initiated. We discussed the possibility that the board would "rest on its laurels" with this unsatisfactory document, which, it could rightly argue, represented a more progressive stance than any other Canadian Board of Education, rather than treating it as a first step to be improved upon in subsequent years. However, the subcommittee finally decided not to take the more radical route, but to endorse the document with the required revisions, including the removal all the material that was incorporated into my work without prior consultation.

The superintendent of curriculum and the board's assistant director were at the April Status of Women Committee meeting to answer questions about the content and process. While much was made of the possibility of "misunderstandings" on the part of "outside" curriculum writers, like myself, who were not board employees, there was some recognition that there had been inadequate consultation, as well as a lack of courtesy, in this instance. Ultimately the staff member who developed the first draft was given responsibility for revising the second draft in accordance with the changes proposed by individuals and groups. The fact that no other curriculum writers—"outside" or otherwise—were brought in to complete these final revisions cast further doubt on the Toronto Board of Education's commitment to community consultation. This time, however, John Campey, an openly gay trustee, had the opportunity to view the third and final draft before it went to the printers.

## Backlash to the Curriculum

A public meeting on the curriculum, chaired by the superintendent of curriculum, was held in May 1992. There were approximately 20 deputations from lesbian and gay groups and allies. In addition, there were in attendance three extremely vocal and virulent right-wing spokesmen, to whom the chair gave free rein to present their hate-filled attacks on gays and lesbians, presumably in the interests of free speech and the much-vaunted "balance."

A well-known right-wing leader subsequently published a half-page advertisement in a national newspaper decrying events at the Toronto Board of Education. He even claimed that what he termed the "psychological abuse" of the board's students through the teaching of the homophobia and sexual orientations curriculum was worse than the sexual abuse of children at Mount Cashel (a school in Newfoundland where young boys had been sexually abused by male teachers). Despite opposition, the June 1992 Board of Education meeting voted in favour of implementing the revised curriculum in the next school year, as well as removing the "proselytization of homosexuality" clause from the policy.

Not surprisingly, the major opposition to this curriculum change came from those parents who correctly perceived the threat to their conservative ideologies posed by lesbian/gay-positive sexuality education: namely, that students might question compulsory heterosexuality and the subordination of women as inevitable. Indeed, it was this kind of community response about which some board staff expressed the greatest concern, presumably because the right wing was perceived as a powerful minority, with direct links to media sources like the *Toronto Sun*. Some staff appeared surprised that the gay and lesbian community failed to express unqualified support for these initiatives.

## Implications for Curriculum Reform

These events provide a clear example of the ways in which conservative forces can dilute and co-opt a progressive community initiative. More cynical observers inside and outside the board expressed the view that the drastic editing procedures were deliberately used to sabotage the success of the proposed curriculum. However, I was somewhat less cynical. In all my interactions with board staff in 1991–1992, I was given the clear message that the speedy completion of the project, hopefully with a minimum of controversy, was of paramount importance. In fact, most staff associated with the curriculum appeared to take pride in this groundbreaking initiative, and anticipated that it would serve as a model for other boards, since requests for copies had already been received from health educators elsewhere in Canada and in the United States. It was therefore difficult to attribute malice or conspiracy to all of those involved, and perhaps it was more appropriate to interpret their behaviour as the actions of liberal pluralists. Personally, I learned a valuable lesson in the frustrations and limitations of trying to work within the system.

Regardless of the motives and interests of board staff, their actions drained the time and energy of members of gay and lesbian community organizations, the Status of Women Committee, and other groups, exacerbated cynicism and burnout among activists, and damaged the board's image of responsiveness to community concerns. Throughout this process, board staff stressed the need to defuse the right-wing backlash, but the possibility of an angry response from left-wing lesbian and gay community groups was not taken seriously. Admittedly, the product was a pioneering curriculum guideline, but the story behind its production demonstrates the shortcomings of liberal social change strategies and the limitations of working within the system.

Reflecting on those events five years later (Lenskyj, 1997), I concluded that there were some positive outcomes. Activists involved in the project estimated that, despite teachers' initial resistance, about 40–50 percent of the Toronto Board of Education's physical and health education staff were using the curriculum guide. They reported that progressive teachers, many of whom were gay or lesbian themselves, saw the guide as opening the door for classroom discussion of sensitive and controversial issues that might not otherwise be aired. Building on the 1989 policy changes, the curriculum represented a significant step in anti-homophobia education in Toronto schools.

CHAPTER 6

# Women's Studies: Feminists Educating Feminists

In 1988, when I first began analyzing feminist pedagogy after four years as a student and two years as a teacher of women's studies, I focused on the social relations of the women's studies classroom, specifically relationships among students, and between the students and instructors (Lenskyj, 1992, 1993, 1994). In the following discussion, I'll reflect on my experiences in the 1980s and 1990s, teaching women's studies in on-campus classrooms in Toronto and in teleconferenced courses with students in northern Ontario.

## Connectedness and Sisterhood

In the 1980s, the major works in women's studies were books such as *Theories of Women's Studies* (Bowles and Klein, 1983), *Learning Our Way* (Bunch and Pollack, 1983), *Gendered Subjects* (Culley and Portuges, 1985), and *Women's Ways of Knowing* (Belenky et al., 1986). These were important catalysts for critically reflecting on the classroom practices and curricula that women's studies instructors were developing, often in isolation from one another. However, many of the early commentaries failed to address issues of power, privilege, and difference based on race, class, and sexuality, and to problematize the ways in which these issues played themselves out between students and instructors, and among students.

Much of the feminist pedagogy literature at this time focused on finding a metaphor that would adequately explain the relationship between feminist instructors and students, with the "mother/daughter" analogy gaining considerable popularity (Culley et al., 1985; Davis, 1985b; Keller and Moglen, 1987; Morgan, 1987). The idea of *connection* was presented as central: specifically, connected teaching and learning, and the "web of connection" in which women live their lives (Belenky et al., 1986; Gilligan, 1982). "Self-in-relation" theories, as developed by Carol Gilligan, Nel Noddings, and others, strongly influenced feminist analyses of women's studies curricula and pedagogy. These theorists explained how female socialization led girls and women to view themselves primarily in relationship to others, in contrast to male socialization toward independence and autonomy. Feminist pedagogy research called for the recognition of connectedness between subject areas through interdisciplinary studies, and between learners, through cooperative rather than competitive learning styles.

At this stage, except for some Black feminist educators such as bell hooks (1988), there was little recognition of the limitations of self-in-relation approaches for feminist pedagogy. Carol Stack (1986) and Joan Tronto (1987) were among the early critics who argued that connectedness was more a function of context and status than of gender, and that members of disadvantaged groups, male as well as female, tended to value interdependence over individualism in order to survive. Furthermore, these critics pointed out that self-in-relation theorists often failed to examine cross-cultural constructions of gender. These kinds of critiques, however, were rarely taken up in feminist pedagogy literature at the time.

Reflecting on my own experiences in women's studies in the 1980s, both as a student and an instructor, I recall that the primary emphasis was on a rather simple notion of sisterhood—in today's terms, we essentialized the category of woman. The element of celebration in these classes was palpable. We were happy to be in a women-only, woman-centred class, perhaps for the first time in our lives, and we did not want to burst that comfortable bubble. But, as Charlotte Bunch and others have pointed out, the idea of sisterhood did not serve all women's interests equally well, and, as a category that encompassed only White, middle-class, heterosexual women, it was not a useful concept. And so, while women's studies classes of the 1980s may have been welcoming to most mainstream women, they were not necessarily so for women from the margins, especially ethnic minority women. The next few years saw the development of more inclusive approaches to feminist, anti-racist, anti-oppression teaching (e.g., Bannerji et al., 1991; O'Malley, 1989; Thompson and Disch, 1992). These discussions were invaluable to feminist instructors who wanted their classes to be places where all women could find their voice.

This is not to suggest that there was only one model of feminist teaching. Discussing "revolutionary feminist pedagogy," bell hooks described how, in teaching Black women's studies, she introduced challenge and confrontation instead of the security and enjoyment that feminist instructors typically cultivated (hooks, 1988). Similarly, Elizabeth Minnich (1983) argued that instructors had a responsibility as critics, not simply as ever-nurturing "mothers," and that feminist education was characterized by struggle, not security. My own position in the 1990s was that it was possible to provide (relative) safety, but not necessarily comfort, in the feminist classroom, and then, as now, I firmly rejected the "mother" role in favour of Minnich's "friends and critics" model.

However, on the issue of safety, it seemed that some women's lives outside the classroom were so fraught with anger and pain that they felt justified in expecting a sanctuary in a women-only classroom, and what was experienced as healthy debate and critique by some was unbearably threatening to others. As a graduate student in some male-dominated courses, my strategy had been to jump into all debates, no matter how heated. I soon realized, however, that some female students felt uncomfortable in these situations and withdrew from the discussion, and I remembered their responses when I began teaching women's studies myself. Although women-only courses generate different debates and dynamics, I agree with bell hooks that there is a place for challenge and confrontation in women's studies classrooms.

## Difference, Diversity, and Power

Barbara Davis's article "Teaching the Feminist Minority" was one of the few in the 1980s to address the question of dynamics between students, specifically, the distance and differences between "new" feminists (more traditional women who are just discovering feminism) and "old" feminists (more radical women who have been politically active for years). As she explained, "The majority [of traditional students] do not know how to support people whose pain is over factions in the women's movement instead of housework" (Davis, 1985a: 248).

There were parallels in classrooms that were ethnically diverse, where, for example, some White women had difficulty understanding why Black women might identify first and foremost with their Black brothers, and not their White sisters (Amos and Parmar, 1984). To acknowledge these realities and to make the bridging process between groups explicit and conscious was crucial to successful feminist teaching. In order to meet the intellectual and emotional needs of new and old feminists, Davis proposed that the instructor act as a "simultaneous translator" by taking the experiential, anecdotal contributions of the "traditional" students and conceptualizing them in feminist terms.

This was no easy task. Some instructors ignored or were unaware of rifts between various groups of students—new and old feminists, lesbian and heterosexual, Black and White, or even feminist and anti-feminist. An instructor may attempt to validate all positions, including misogynist, racist, and homophobic stances, in the misguided belief that the feminist classroom has to be comfortable and open to all, bigots included. Alternatively, a more dogmatic or forceful instructor may inadvertently silence some students by her espousal of a particular position, or by her unconscious siding with one group against another. Or, looking for some middle ground, an instructor may acknowledge that students are in different places on their personal journeys, and may state explicitly that openness and tolerance of difference are required of all students. But, at the same time, the instructor knows that not all positions *are* equally valid.

Women's studies instructors can expect non-feminist students to respect the feminist perspective that animates the class. Such students should not assume they can take up class time with capricious challenges: women aren't oppressed; incest doesn't happen; this course is biased against men. The instructor then faces a dilemma as she uses her power in ways that appear antithetical to the democratic principle of feminist process, in order to salvage the learning experience for the other students. Feminist instructors have argued convincingly against abusing the power of the instructor's role (Friedman, 1985; Maher, 1985). Using Paulo Freire's insights, however, it is possible to distinguish between authoritative behaviour that is justified by the instructor's intellectual authority, and authoritarian behaviour that is an abuse of power. I can recall situations where some students expected me to use my power to rescue them from domineering students, or to support what they saw as their "correct" stance on an issue. For my part, I expected all participants to share the responsibility for classroom dynamics, even in difficult situations like these, but I was ready to intervene on the basis of intellectual authority.

A feminist instructor, I believe, is justified in challenging racism, classism, homophobia, heterosexism, and other forms of oppression, and in expecting all students to grapple with their personal prejudices and fears of difference, as she herself is doing. However, the issue of lesbian-heterosexual rifts between students presented unique problems, particularly in the 1980s when the climate on university campuses was less tolerant than it is today. Whereas a White, middle-class instructor could support working-class or Black students with no threat to her own class position or ethnic identity, a heterosexual feminist instructor who supported lesbian students or challenged homophobic comments might be suspected of being lesbian, especially given the common tendency to conflate lesbian with feminist. And an instructor who *was* lesbian might view the risks of coming out as unacceptably high, particularly in mainstream academic settings that were not renowned for their acceptance of feminism, let alone lesbianism. Academic "gate-keepers"—traditionally White, heterosexual men—who made decisions about tenure and promotion, grant applications, and publications had considerable power over the careers of female faculty. Some instructors who were known to be lesbian also experienced discrimination and sexual harassment. However, on the question of professors staying "in the closet," I agree with Paula Bennett's assertion, made more than 20 years ago: "To betray oneself in this way for a [university] job is certainly not a price worth paying" (Bennett, 1982: 7).

Since the risks for lesbian students and instructors are high, it seems reasonable to expect supportive heterosexual women to join lesbians in identifying and challenging homophobia and heterosexism. One outcome of disclosing one's lesbianism is that one is expected to assume the role of "resident expert" on lesbian issues ("What do you think causes lesbianism, Helen?") and the monitor of heterosexist and homophobic content. As an instructor who routinely makes this disclosure to students, I find it very heartening to see heterosexual women sharing the responsibility for identifying heterosexist bias in class discussions or student presentations, so that lesbians are no longer the only voices raising consciousness on these issues.

## Women's Studies from a Distance

With the expansion of women's studies programs in the 1980s, feminist instructors began to use distance education to reach students who had limited access to college- and university-based courses because of their geographic location, especially those living in Canada's North. In Ontario, Contact North/Contact nord, a telecommunications network in Sudbury, was an important component of post-secondary distance education.

In 1988, after two years of teaching graduate courses in women's studies at the Ontario Institute for Studies in Education (OISE), I presented the first teleconferenced distance course in the women's studies specialization—a sociology course entitled "Women and the Educational System" (see Burge and Lenskyj, 1990). I later taught two other distance courses, one on feminist perspectives in education, and the other on women's health movements and the health professions. With the exception of one women's history course, these were OISE's only women's studies courses offered by distance mode in the 1980s and early 1990s.

In the eight years that I taught women's studies by distance mode, about 90 percent of the students were women. Most students were in the part-time M.Ed. program, and most had full-time jobs in teaching (elementary, secondary, and post-secondary levels), nursing, or social work. In contrast, on-campus courses had many full-time students, and those who were employed worked in a wider range of occupations than the distance students.

Every distance student received a package of materials before the first class: a learner's manual, a set of readings, audio cassettes, and materials listing feminist resources, including publications of OISE's Centre for Women's Studies in Education. Most students participated in the weekly teleconference at a local site—a school or community college—where a microphone/speaker system linked them to the other participants and to the instructor. Depending on their location, students might be alone or in a small group at the local site. Those who lived too far from the site phoned from home—as one woman described herself, sitting in her favourite armchair with a cup of coffee. Through the Contact North telecommunications operator, it was possible to have small group as well as large group discussion, with or without the instructor on the line.

As noted above, by the late 1980s, some educational research was addressing issues of authority and social relations in the feminist classroom. At this time, a few books and articles were examining the general question of women in distance education, as well as the specific issue of feminist pedagogy in distance learning.[5] However, even in later research on feminist distance education, there was a tendency to speak of "women" as an undifferentiated category and to present connectedness too deterministically as a gender-*specific*, rather than a gender-*related* approach (e.g., Bowman and Will, 1994).

Women's studies by distance mode present unique pedagogical challenges to the feminist teacher. She may never meet her students face to face, and they may never see each other, except through an exchange of photographs. During a teleconference, she has to facilitate discussions among disembodied voices and to interpret silences as well as voices. How can she tune in to the often highly charged climate of the feminist classroom in the absence of visual signals? How can she function without eye contact and non-verbal messages that convey the wide ranges of emotions generated in these courses? How can she understand the everyday lives of women living in remote regions of Canada, and the specific challenges facing Indigenous women? And how can she do the bridge-building that is crucial to the feminist classroom: making connections between women while making conscious their social class, ethnic, and sexual differences, as well as their differing levels of feminist awareness and political experiences?

Even though distance learning opened up the possibility for students outside of major urban centres to participate in a valuable learning experience, I found that the absence of face-to-face encounters was a barrier to total engagement between students and instructor, and among the students themselves. As Karlene Faith (1988) pointed out, the technology tended to make distance education individualistic, whereas many women preferred collaborative learning. This presented challenges for feminist instructors teaching women's studies, where both the process and the content were by definition controversial and issue-laden, and where sustained discussion and interaction were crucial to the learning process. However, the teleconference, unlike today's computer-mediated instruction, at least allowed for real-time conversations.

I have a theory that women are generally well suited to telephone-conferencing. Many women have a long-standing relationship with the telephone and have developed the ability to read emotions and personality indicators conveyed by voice alone. Therefore, I expected that the feminist pedagogical approaches I had developed in face-to-face classrooms could effectively be adapted to suit distance classes. My theory was to some extent substantiated, and most students expressed considerable comfort with telephone-conferencing and satisfaction with their learning. The feminist component of the courses contributed to students' positive experiences, with the most enthusiastic course evaluations reflecting growing feminist consciousness. One woman told the group that she had never spoken out in a teleconference discussion, unless called upon to do so, in any of her preceding seven courses, but in this course she was a keen participant.

However, some women reported that the mode of communication was occasionally frustrating when lively discussions were taking place. Only one person could speak at a time (because of the technology), and it was not always clear who had the floor. One solution was for me to invite responses by naming each student, but this interfered with the spontaneity and flow. Although distance mode made it easy for a student who felt alienated or silenced simply to withdraw, very few students did. Those who were potentially the most likely to be alienated—a small number of male students—usually participated in a non-confrontational and open manner, and, like many of the female students, showed considerable personal and intellectual growth during the course.

On the negative side, distance mode also made it possible for students to come to class without completing pre-class readings and discussion questions. It became clear from a disgruntled student's course evaluation that, in one small group discussion, a few students impeded progress because of their frequent lack of preparation and their tendency to digress. However, many female students experienced a triple workday as employees, wives/mothers, and students, some had unsupportive male partners, while others were struggling to succeed in male-defined career paths. For these women, resolving the perennial problem of lack of time was difficult.

For me, one source of frustration during the early stages of teaching by distance mode involved not knowing when to stop explaining complex or controversial topics—not knowing whether students were convinced, bored, struggling to understand, or more deeply entrenched in their original position. Some appeared to believe that racism, homophobia, and violence against women and children were urban phenomena, and I sensed that many viewed me as the classic urban radical feminist, out of touch with the realities of life in northern Ontario. While I challenged many of these assumptions, I did acknowledge the urban-centric bias of many of the readings in the first course, and I broadened the geographic scope in future materials, as well as visiting some centres in the north to meet students face to face. More importantly, girls' and women's lives in northern Ontario became the raw material for class discussion and analysis, course assignments, and final papers, as I encouraged students to personalize their responses to all the issues and topics covered in the course. As was the case with on-campus students, many women experienced these links between the personal and the political as exciting and empowering.

Quite early in my distance teaching experience, I attempted to put the general race and ethnicity issues, as well as Indigenous issues, on the agenda near the beginning of each course. For example, an activity scheduled for the second day required each student to provide a short sketch of her or his mother's educational experiences, or those of a woman of the same generation as their mothers. I included this option in case a student found the other too personal or threatening; a few students chose to talk about a family friend, rather than their mothers, and were not expected to defend this choice. I also participated in the activity myself by telling my own mother's story.

This sharing of stories served several purposes. Firstly, it enabled students to disclose aspects of their ethnic and class backgrounds to the extent they felt safe in doing so, without focusing attention on themselves. In a typical distance course of about eight students, at least one came from an ethnic minority background. Secondly, it provided an avenue for male as well as female participants to contribute to a woman-centred and woman-affirming climate in the group; and, lastly, it gave participants a way of integrating the real-life educational experiences of women they knew into the actual content of the course. On every occasion that I used it, it was a moving experience for all participants, with numerous accounts of incredible hardship and courage on the part of women of earlier generations, many of whom were immigrants to Canada. Moreover, we often came back to our mothers' stories at other points in the course as we discussed factors influencing women's education, such as violence and poverty.

I should note, in passing, that I didn't find the technique of circulating students' photographs to be an effective way of raising issues of race and ethnicity, although it served other purposes. There were invariably a number of students who did not provide photographs for a variety of reasons related, I suspect, to privacy and self-image. Indeed, for the many women who have a negative self-image, distance courses offered a kind of anonymity. Several years ago, one of my female students explained to the group that she did not circulate a photograph of herself because she just wanted the others to "see" her based on what she said and how she said it. Toward the end of the course, she told the group that she was South Asian. When we subsequently met in person, it was also clear that she was an attractive woman, and so my theory about self-image did not hold true for her; rather, she was concerned about prejudice based on her ethnic identity.

My own subject position as a White, middle-class, lesbian instructor forced me to confront another major question of difference. Throughout my university teaching, most of my on-campus women's studies courses included at least one or two (openly) lesbian, gay, or bisexual participants. In additional, there were usually some non-lesbian students whose extensive community-based political work had familiarized them with issues of homophobia and heterosexism, and had brought them in contact with lesbians and gay men.

In the broader social context, Ontario was one of the first provinces to include sexual orientation as prohibited grounds for discrimination, and OISE had for many years provided same-sex spousal benefits to its employees. While these conditions did not guarantee that discussions of sexual difference would proceed without problem in OISE classrooms, lesbian/gay instructors and students were more secure than many of their counterparts in other universities and other provinces. However, in my distance courses, only one student disclosed a lesbian/gay identity and no one referred to lesbian or gay friends or family members. In smaller towns, where "everyone knew everyone," it was often dangerous for gays and lesbians to be public about their sexuality, and so they either sought the anonymity of a larger city or kept their sexuality secret. As a result, many heterosexual people living in small communities could say, with apparent certainty, that they didn't know any gays or lesbians. This kind of assertion was common in many of the public debates surrounding attempts to introduce provincial legislation on same-sex spousal benefits in the early 1990s when right-wing opponents portrayed homosexuality as "a Toronto problem."

Teaching women's studies by teleconference, I soon recognized how much I depended on face-to-face feedback in order to assess my effectiveness. Students' facial expressions and body language conveyed much about their readiness for or resistance to the ideas that I was presenting, and in view of the fact that women's studies is by definition a project of consciousness raising, controversial ideas were commonplace. I probably wasted a lot of time unnecessarily prolonging my side of the debate when the student had tuned out some time before. Conversely, students in a teleconference were unable to assess my emotional reaction to their comments, and so, to address this problem, I chose to make my reaction very clear, for example, through my tone of voice and choice of words, or through explicitly stating what I was feeling. For example, I would say, "I was smiling while you were saying that because ... " or "I want to say this gently, but I think you should consider ... " or "I feel awkward saying this ... "

## The Down Side: Homophobia and Bigotry

This brings me to a situation that I confronted at a point about midway in the "Feminist Perspectives" course when the readings and class discussion focused on issues of sexual difference, homophobia, and heterosexism. I had planned, as was my practice at the time, to say explicitly on that night that I was lesbian. I usually made indirect references to the fact quite early in the course, for example, by talking about gay and lesbian issues in the first-person plural, using the pronoun "we" rather than "they." Indeed, in the 1980s, the inclusion of any lesbian content in a course usually suggested to students that the instructor was lesbian or lesbian-positive in her politics.

On this occasion, before I could make my disclosure, a female student whose voice I didn't recognize made a statement to the effect that, while she was okay with gay men, she "couldn't stand lesbians." Her tone indicated that this was a deeply held position. I immediately intervened, saying something like, "I should tell you at this point that I'm lesbian, and it's difficult to talk about this, particularly following that statement, when I can't see people's faces .... " I went on to explain how the issue fitted into the themes of the course, and there was no more discussion of a personal nature on that night or in subsequent classes. Ever since that incident, my policy has always been to come out on the *first* day of the course—not exactly

"My name is Helen and I'm a lesbian," but some equally unambiguous statement!

No doubt the student in question, and others, felt embarrassed, and my intervention was timed so that she could not further embarrass herself. More importantly, suffering an acute reaction somewhere in the pit of my stomach, I had to intervene for my own survival. I knew, too, that any more prejudiced statements on her part would cause pain to others who were gay or lesbian, or who had gay or lesbian family members or friends, and so I felt justified in using my power as instructor, constrained as it was by my minority position as lesbian, to speak out. There may have been students who wanted to challenge her too, but feared that doing so might label them lesbian or gay, particularly if they lived in a conservative community. On a similar note, a heterosexual student once wrote to me about the political climate in the small town where he lived. No one, he said, shared his liberal views about gender and other equity issues, and he found the class discussions and the opportunity to read and write about social justice issues extremely liberating.

I now turn to another example of a student response that was in part a result of the absence of face-to-face interaction in distance courses. In addition to a final paper for the course, students were asked to complete two or three short response papers that critiqued course readings, to be sent to me in the first two months. This enabled me to identity potential problems before students started work on their final papers. I encouraged them to integrate personal experience and perspective where this was appropriate. In other words, I wasn't looking for a summary of the reading, but rather for a personal response informed by the other readings and class discussions, and I stated these expectations clearly in the learners' manual.

One response paper came from a White female teacher living in northern Ontario. On the first page, she launched into an attack—largely unrelated to the article she was evaluating—on a local educational program for children with special needs. From this inauspicious beginning, the paper degenerated into a vicious, victim-blaming tirade against virtually every disadvantaged group in society. Older women, she stated, should "get some initiative and fend for themselves," not "sit around and mope," and non-English-speaking immigrant women "should learn the language." Women in low-paying jobs shouldn't have "made a decision that education was not necessary," and parents of disabled children shouldn't receive "any more money" in government allowances than other parents did. She reserved her harshest criticism for teen mothers, who, in her estimation, were either "stupid" for getting pregnant in the first place, or were exploiting their single motherhood status to get access to "taxpayers' money" in order to live a life of ease. Lesbians were one of the few groups to escape her censure.

Needless to say, I was stunned by this paper, which, in addition to its victim-blaming assertions, relied on unsubstantiated assumptions and lacked even a basic understanding and application of sociological analysis. Rather than commenting extensively on substantive problems, which was my first reaction, I sent the student a carefully worded letter explaining my general expectations for the paper, reiterating and expanding on the directions in the learners' manual, and requesting her to submit a completely new paper. If I had failed her first assignment, she would probably have dropped the course in order to avoid a low final grade, and would have missed the rest of the class discussions and readings on equity issues. In her subsequent written work for the course, she avoided any controversial issues and, I suspect, suppressed any personal opinions. In other words, I managed to change her behaviour—an important first step—but probably not her attitude. There would have been a different, and probably more satisfactory, outcome if this had been an on-campus course with face-to-face interaction.

Comparing my experiences of on-campus and distance teaching, I observed differences in students' behaviour. For example, the two situations described above, where students apparently believed that it was appropriate to voice the most profound bigotry, were never replicated in an on-campus course. This was not necessarily because there were no Toronto students who shared such sentiments. I suspect that students from the Toronto area, who form the majority in on-campus women's studies classes, were sufficiently exposed to the diversity debates at least to self-monitor their spoken or written views in order to be perceived as fitting into OISE's liberal subculture. In other words, they were perhaps too guarded and "sophisticated" (in the negative sense of the word) to make offensive statements publicly, even though their underlying attitudes may have been classist, racist, or homophobic.

This is not to suggest that the backlash did not manifest itself in downtown Toronto, where students often attacked the so-called "political correctness" movement on campuses—more accurately, the movement for equity and inclusiveness. These backlash views were often expressed in the language of progressive social movements, and on a few occasions my colleagues and I were covertly accused, in students' course evaluations and elsewhere, of "silencing" free speech and "discriminating" against White, middle-class students.

Some northern Ontario students, on the other hand, had less exposure to diversity debates and were less likely to self-monitor their views. This tendency enabled me, as instructor, to understand their current awareness level and to respond appropriately. For example, in the late 1980s when there was controversy over a provincial government job posting that gave priority to non-White applicants, a female student told the class how her husband had once hired a Native man, who, she claimed, was an incompetent worker—thereby proving that priority hiring was "a bad idea."

Subsequent discussion of affirmative action and tokenism proved to be an effective learning opportunity. In another example, a student who worked as a nurse challenged the arguments presented in an article on racism in nursing, and attempted to rationalize a well-documented racist incident from a nurse management perspective. This in turn prompted a discussion of systemic racism as well as individual practices that may have racist outcomes.

## Conclusion

The 1980s and 1990s were challenging times in the development of women's studies. In reflecting on my own experiences in on-campus and distance courses, I can see how a kind of pioneering spirit motivated both students and instructors as we celebrated the achievements of the first generation of graduates specializing in women's studies. At the same time, feminist instructors recognized that the mainstream university continued to entrench systems of privilege and power, regardless of our first steps toward transforming curriculum and pedagogy. Like it or not, we were working within the system, and to take a radical feminist approach was "to live the contradictions."

# Final Reflections

Although there have been significant changes in the education of girls and women since my mother's childhood, and since my own, much has stayed the same. Sydney's private schools continue to be populated largely by the sons and daughters of the ruling class, while public education suffers the ill effects of inadequate funding.

In the 1980s and 1990s, curriculum and program initiatives aimed at enhancing the education of girls, particularly those in the public school system, were perceived by some as "too successful." When girls began to outperform boys in some subjects in the standardized High School Certificate examinations, there was widespread backlash, and the "What about the boys?" movement, supported by some powerful male academics, threatened many of the hard-won gains in girls' education (Foster et al., 2003).

The gap between the rich and poor in Sydney is symbolized geographically by the great divide between the wealthy eastern suburbs, where Kambala is located, and Sydney's western suburbs, where my mother stayed with her sister Doris in 1918. Today, western suburbs residents are mostly working-class and immigrant families, and these "Westies," particularly Lebanese and Vietnamese youth, are all routinely portrayed as criminals in the mainstream media (Poynting, 2000). In many respects, the life chances of girls in Sydney's western suburbs today are not markedly different from those of previous generations: early school leaving, dead-end jobs, and, for many, single parenthood.

In Toronto, the Board of Education's efforts at democratizing decision making, prompted by radical community initiatives of the 1970s and 1980s, waned in the 1990s. Structural changes in 1997, engineered by the neo-conservative provincial government, resulted in the amalgamation of five Toronto area school boards into a new "mega-board"—the Toronto District School Board (TDSB)—and the disempowerment of trustees, parents, and communities.

On the issue of homophobia in the schools, "religious accommodation" provisions in TDSB equity policies were used by some parents from right-wing religious groups to justify their virulent opposition to initiatives aimed at recognizing sexual orientation as a designated equity area. Along with other objections, opponents erroneously characterized the homophobia and sexual orientations curriculum guide discussed in Chapter 5 as a document that provided instruction only on *homo*sexual orientation, and proceeded to oppose the teaching of this curriculum in the schools as a violation of their religious freedom (Fumia, 2003). One positive note: in 2000, the Anti-Homophobia Equity Committee, established by a group of interested teachers, parents, and community people in 1998, was recognized, after considerable struggle, as a formal committee of TDSB.

Finally, in the area of university women's studies programs, the forced merger of OISE (now renamed OISE/UT) with the University of Toronto in 1996 undermined some aspects of its distinctive culture as a pioneer in women's studies and anti-oppression teaching. The merger also resulted in an end to the unionized status of former OISE faculty and the introduction of more quantitative approaches to faculty evaluation—for many feminist and lesbian instructors, changes that did little to enhance personal or professional security.

## FINAL REFLECTIONS

Positive changes, particularly in my own department, Sociology and Equity Studies in Education (SESE), included significantly more ethnic diversity among both students and faculty, and the heightened expectation on the part of most, but not all, instructors that equity studies must incorporate an analysis of *all* systems of oppression, including homophobia and heterosexism. Yet, while some openly lesbian candidates have been appointed to other OISE/UT departments, there have been none among the new appointments to SESE since 1996.

On the first day of any of my women's studies courses, I can expect to see a diverse group of students in terms of age and ethnicity. As the course proceeds, less visible aspects of diversity—social class, ability, sexuality—are often disclosed. Alliances form across these lines, but the divide between the "old" and "new" feminists discussed in Chapter 6 is often the most difficult to cross. In some ways, teaching women's studies becomes easier, while in other ways, it never becomes easy. As my mother would say, "We have a lot to learn."

# Endnotes

[1] The scholarly convention would be to refer to her as "Hawthorne," but I've always thought of her as "Miss Hawthorne" and have retained this term because it fits better with my personal narrative.

[2] I'm using pseudonyms and removing identifying features because both women are now deceased and I cannot get permission to reveal their identities.

[3] Some sections of Chapter 4 are based on papers I completed for undergraduate education courses and on newspaper clippings that I saved in the 1970s. As a result, many sources lack dates and page numbers. Where this is the case, I've provided all the available information in the text and omitted these incomplete references from the bibliography.

[4] At this time, the terms "gay" and "lesbian" were commonly used to denote the sexual minorities who, more recently, would be referred to as lesbian, gay, bisexual, and transgendered people. Here, I'm employing the terms that were used when these events were taking place.

[5] The first anthology on this topic, *Toward New Horizons: International Perspectives on Women and Distance Education*, edited by Karlene Faith, appeared in 1988, and the Canadian *Journal of Distance Education* published a special issue on women (vol. 5, no. 2) in 1990. Other relevant articles were published in Canadian journals and anthologies around the same time (see, for example, Bray, 1988; Burge, 1991; Burge and Lenskyj, 1990; Coulter, 1989).

# Bibliography

Ainsworth, M. 1972. "The Author—an Appreciation." In *Kambala: A History* by F. Hawthorne. Sydney: Wentworth Press.

Amos, V., and P. Parmar. 1984. "Challenging Imperial Feminism." *Feminist Review* 17: 3–19.

Anderson, D. 1990. "The Public/Private Division in Australian Schooling: Social and Education Effects." In *Schooling and Society in Australia*, edited by L. Saha and K. Keeves, 87–110. Sydney: Australian National University Press.

Angus, C., A. Kerr, and H. Lenskyj. 1991. Critique of Dr. Ron Langevin's presentation, "No more victims, no more victimizers: Youth violence prevention." Paper presented to the Status of Women Committee, Toronto Board of Education.

Area Four Curriculum Council. 1975. Minutes of meeting (April 16).

Arnstein, S. 1969. "A Ladder of Citizen Participation." *American Institute of Planners Journal* 35, no. 4: 216–224.

Baird, J., and G. Noonan. 2000. "A Loosening of the Old School Tie." *Sydney Morning Herald* (January 29): 11.

Bannerji, H., L. Carty, K. Dehli, S. Heald, and K. McKenna. 1991. *Unsettling Relations: The University as Site of Feminist Struggles*. Toronto: Women's Press.

Belenky, M., B. Clinchy, N. Goldberger, and J. Tarule. 1986. *Women's Ways of Knowing*. New York: Basic Books.

Bell, D. 1987. *Generations*. Fitzroy: McPhee Gribble/Penguin.

Bennett, P. 1982. "Dyke in Academe (II)." In *Lesbian Studies*, edited by M. Cruikshank, 3–8. Old Westbury: Feminist Press.

Blizzard, C. 1990. "Stick to Council Matters." *Toronto Sun* (November 16): 27.

Bowles, G., and R. Klein. 1983. *Theories of Women's Studies*. London: Routledge & Kegan Paul.

Bowman, A., and R. Will. 1994. "Distance Education for Women: Peril or Possibility?" In *Feminism and Education*, edited by P. Bourne, P. Masters, N. Amin, M. Gonick, and L. Gribowski, 65–80. Toronto: Centre for Women's Studies in Education, Ontario Institute for Studies in Education.

Bray, C. 1988. "Women's Studies at a Distance: Experiences of Student and Tutor." *Canadian Journal of University Continuing Education* 14, no. 2: 37–49.

Bryson, L. 1994. "Women, Paid Work and Social Policy." In *Australian Women: Contemporary Feminist Thought*, edited by N. Grieve and A. Burns, 179–193. Melbourne: Oxford University Press.

Bunch, C., and S. Pollack. 1983. *Learning Our Way*. Trumansburg: Crossing Press.

Burge, E. 1991. "Women as Learners: Issues for Visual and Virtual Classrooms." *Canadian Journal for the Study of Adult Education* 4, no. 2: 1–24.

Burge, E., and H. Lenskyj. 1990. "Women Studying in Distance Education: Issues and Principles." *Journal of Distance Education* 5, no. 1: 20–37.

Burgmann, V., and J. Lee. 1988. *Making a Life: A People's History of Australia Since 1788*. Fitzroy: McPhee Gribble/Penguin.

## BIBLIOGRAPHY

Burns, A. 1986. "Why Do Women Continue to Marry?" In *Australian Women: New Feminist Perspectives*, edited by N. Grieve and A. Burns, 210–232. Melbourne: Oxford University Press.

Burrows, D. 1968. *History of Abbotsleigh*. Wahroonga: Council of Abbotsleigh.

Capp, F. 2004. "Yanking the Old School Tie." *The Age* (June 5) <www.theage.com.au>.

Chow, O. 1986. "Report to School Programs Committee, Policies and Programs Regarding Sexual Orientation, and Notice of Motion to Toronto Board of Education School Programs Committee" (April 6).

Collins, P. 1991. "On Our Own Terms: Self-defined Standpoints and Curriculum Transformation." *National Women's Studies Association Journal* 3, no. 3: 367–381.

Connell, R., D. Ashenden, S. Kessler, and G. Dowsett. 1982. *Making a Difference: Schools, Families and Social Division*. North Sydney: Allen & Unwin Australia.

Conway, J. 1990. *The Road from Coorain*. London: Mandarin.

———. 1994. *True North*. Toronto: Knopf.

———. 2001. *A Woman's Education*. New York: Random House.

Conway, J., ed. 1999. "Introduction." In *In Her Own Words: Women's Memoirs from Australia, New Zealand, Canada and the United States*, vii–xi. New York: Vintage.

Coulter, R. 1989. "Women and Distance Education: Towards a Feminist Perspective." In *Postsecondary Distance Education in Canada: Policies, Practices and Priorities*, edited by R. Sweet, 11–22. Edmonton: Athabasca.

Crotty, M. 2003. "Pointing the Way—Antipodean Responses to J.A. Mangan's *Athleticism* and Related Studies: Scotch College, Melbourne, in the Inter-war Years." *International Journal of History of Sport* 20, no. 4: 64–81.

Culley, M., A. Diamond, L. Edwards, S. Lennox, and C. Portuges. 1985. "The Politics of Nurturance." In *Gendered Subjects*, edited by M. Culley and C. Portuges, 11–20. London: Routledge & Kegan Paul.

Culley, M., and C. Portuges, eds. 1985. *Gendered Subjects: The Dynamics of Feminist Teaching.* London: Routledge & Kegan Paul.

Davidson, R. 1987. "The Mythological Crucible." In *Australia: Beyond the Dreamtime*, by T. Keneally, P. Adam-Smith, and R. Davidson, 169–240. London: BBC Books.

Davis, B. 1985a. "Teaching the Feminist Minority." In *Gendered Subjects*, edited by M. Culley and C. Portuges, 245–252. London: Routledge & Kegan Paul.

Davis, B., ed. 1985b. "Feminist Education." Special edition of *The Journal of Thought* 20: 3.

Davis, T. 2003. "How to ... Drive a Bus." *Sydney Morning Herald* (December 23) <www.smh.com.au>.

Dehli, K., and I. Januario. 1994. *Parent Activism and School Reform in Toronto.* Toronto: Department of Sociology in Education, Ontario Institute for Studies in Education.

Dehli, K., J. Restakis, and E. Sharpe. 1988. "The Rise and Fall of the Parent Movement in Toronto." In *Social Movements, Social Change*, edited by F. Cunningham, S. Findlay, M. Kadar, A. Lennon, and E. Silva, 290–227. Toronto: Between the Lines.

Dixson, M. 1976. *The Real Matilda: Women and Identity in Australia 1788 to the Present.* Ringwood: Penguin.

Editorial. 1951. *Kambala Chronicle* (unpublished notes). Box 252, AGC 98, Kambala Archives.

Education in Downtown Toronto. 1972. Laneway Community School.

Faith, K., ed. 1988. *Toward New Horizons: International Perspectives on Women and Distance Education.* London: Routledge.

Finch, L. 1990. "Seduction and Punishment." *Hecate* 16, no. 1/2: 8–22.

Foster, J. 1985. *Sex Variant Women in Literature*. Tallahassee: Naiad (first published 1956, Vantage).

Foster, V., M. Kimmel, and C. Skelton. 2003. "'What about the Boys?' An Overview of the Debates." In *What about the Boys?*, edited by W. Martino and B. Meyenn, 1–23. Buckingham: Open University Press.

Frankland Community Council. 1972. Minutes of meeting (May 17).

Friedman, S. 1985. "Authority in the Feminist Classroom: A Contradiction in Terms?" In *Gendered Subjects*, edited by M. Culley and C. Portuges, 203–208. London: Routledge & Kegan Paul.

Fumia, D. 2003. "Competing for a Piece of the Pie: Equity Seeking and the Toronto District School Board in the 1990s." Ph.D. dissertation, Ontario Institute for Studies in Education, University of Toronto.

Gay Fathers' Chapter, Gay and Lesbian Parents' Coalition. 1991. Letter to Ouida Wright, Superintendent of Curriculum (May 13).

Gill, J. 1995. "Girls and Schools: A Layering of Past Experience and Present Positioning." Paper presented to the annual conference of the Australian Association of Research in Education, Hobart, Tasmania (November) <www.aare.edu.au/95pap/gillj95.268>.

Gilligan, C. 1982. *In a Different Voice*. Cambridge: Harvard University Press.

Glasson, W. 1941. "Our Shepherds." Unpublished booklet, copied by hand by Doris McOnie, July 24, 1972.

Godden, J. 1979. "A New Look at Pioneer Women." *Hecate* V, no. 2: 6–21.

God's Enforcers. 2003. *The Justice Project: The Abuse of Children in Care*. Brisbane: University of Queensland <www.eastes.net/justiceproject/htm/TheCatAndTheWhip.asp>.

Grieve, N., and A. Burns, eds. 1986. *Australian Women: New Feminist Perspectives*. Melbourne: Oxford University Press.

———, eds. 1986. "Introduction." In *Australian Women: New Feminist Perspectives*, edited by N. Grieve and A. Burns, 1–13. Melbourne: Oxford University Press.

———, eds. 1994. *Australian Women: Contemporary Feminist Thought*. Melbourne: Oxford University Press.

Grimshaw, P. 1986. "'Man's Own Country': Women in Colonial Australian History." In *Australian Women: New Feminist Perspectives*, edited by N. Grieve and A. Burns, 182–209. Melbourne: Oxford University Press.

Hamilton, P. 1990. "'Inventing the Self': Oral History as Autobiography." *Hecate* 16, no. 1/2: 128–133.

Harris, D. 1988. "A Great Ring of Landlords?" In *Making a Life*, edited by V. Burgmann and J. Lee, 39–55. Fitzroy: McPhee Gribble/Penguin.

Hawthorne, F. 1972. *Kambala: A History*. Sydney: Wentworth Press.

Henry, M. 1996. *Parent-School Collaboration: Feminist Organization Structures and School Leadership*. Albany: SUNY.

Hogan, M. 1984. *Public vs. Private Schools*. Ringwood: Penguin.

hooks, b. 1988. *Talking Back*. Toronto: Between the Lines.

Johnson, L. 1993. *The Modern Girl: Girlhood and Growing Up*. St. Leonards: Allen & Unwin.

Keating, D. 1975. *The Power to Make It Happen*. Toronto: Green Tree Press.

———. 1979. "The Future of Neighbourhood Organizing." In *Participatory Democracy in Action*, edited by D. Chekki, 227–246. Sahibabad: Vika.

Keller, E., and H. Moglen. 1987. "Competition: A Problem for Academic Women." In *Competition: A Feminist Taboo?*, edited by H. Longino and V. Miner, 21–37. New York: Feminist Press.

Keneally, T. 1987. "Here Nature Is Reversed." In *Australia: Beyond the Dreamtime*, by T. Keneally, P. Adam-Smith, and R. Davidson, 11–80. London: BBC Books.

Keneally, T., P. Adam-Smith, and R. Davidson. 1987. *Australia: Beyond the Dreamtime*. London: BBC Books.

Kyle, N. 1986. *Her Natural Destiny*. Kensington: University of NSW Press.

Laneway Community School. 1972. Submission to Toronto Board of Education (March 9).

Langley, E. [1942] 1991. *The Pea Pickers*. Sydney: Angus & Robertson.

Lenskyj, H. 1986. *Out of Bounds: Women, Sport and Sexuality*. Toronto: Women's Press.

———. 1991. "Mothers, Daughters, Wives: Three Generations of Australian Women." Paper presented at the Annual Meeting of the Canadian Sociology and Anthropology Association, Kingston, Ontario.

———. 1992. "Tele-communication: Women's Studies through Distance Education." *Resources for Feminist Research* 20, no. 1/2: 11–12.

———. 1993. "The Politics of Feminist Pedagogy: Implications for Teaching Women in the Human Services Professions." In *Weaving Alliances*, edited by D. Martens, 35–46. Ottawa: Canadian Women's Studies Association.

———. 1994. "Commitment and Compromise: Feminist Pedagogy in the Academy." In *Feminism and Education: A Canadian Perspective*, vol. 2, edited by P. Bourne, P. Masters, N. Amin, M. Gonick, and L. Gribowski, 3–15. Toronto: Centre for Women's Studies in Education, Ontario Institute for Studies in Education.

———. 1997. "Changing Sex Education." *Orbit* 28, no. 1: 18–20.

———. 2002. *The Best Olympics Ever? Social Impacts of Sydney 2000*. Albany: SUNY.

*Life Events Index.* 2003. Compiled for the Molong Historical Society <www2.tpg.com.au/users/mackenzy/me1880s.html>.

Lind, L. 1971. "Toronto Abolishes the Strap." *Globe and Mail* (July 23).

———. 1974. *The Learning Machine.* Toronto: House of Anansi Press.

Lorimer, J. 1969. "The Mothers Who Want to Change the School System." *Globe and Mail* (August 25): 7.

Maher, F. 1985. "Classroom Pedagogy and the New Scholarship on Women." In *Gendered Subjects,* edited by M. Culley and C. Portuges, 29–48. London: Routledge & Kegan Paul.

Mahood, L. 2002. "'Give Him a Doing': The Birching of Young Offenders in Scotland." *Canadian Journal of History* 37, no. 3: 439–457.

Markey, R. 1980. "Women and Labour, 1880–1900." In *Women, Class and History,* edited by E. Windschuttle, 83–111. Melbourne: Fontana.

Martell, G. 1970. "Community Control of the Schools in New York and Toronto." *This Magazine Is about Schools* 4, no. 3: 6–49.

———. 1971. "The Community School Workshop in Toronto." *This Magazine Is about Schools* 5, no. 2: 74–84.

Matthews, J. 1984. *Good and Mad Women.* North Sydney: Allen & Unwin.

McCalman, J. 1993. *Journeyings: The Biography of a Middle-Class Generation 1920–1990.* Melbourne: Melbourne University Press.

McCaskell, T., and T. Gambini. 1990. Letter to Ouida Wright, Superintendent of Curriculum (October 29).

McGregor, C. 2001. *Class in Australia.* Ringwood: Penguin.

McIntosh, P. 1983. "Interactive Phases of Curriculum Revision." Wellesley College Centre for Research on Women, *Working Papers Series.*

Melaun, K. 1954. "Here's Your Answer." *Australian Women's Weekly* (June 23): 35.

Middleton, S. 1993. *Educating Feminists: Life Histories and Pedagogy.* New York: Teachers College Press, Columbia University.

Ministry of Education, Ontario. 1987. *Education about AIDS.* Toronto: Ministry of Education.

Minnich, E. 1983. "Friends and Critics: The Feminist Academy." In *Learning Our Way*, edited by C. Bunch and S. Pollack, 317–330. Trumansburg: Crossing Press.

*Molong Express.* Obituary, Mrs. Mary Kerr Evers. 1956. *The Molong Express* (July 13).

*Molong Express.* Untitled clipping. 1989. *The Molong Express* (December 1).

Morgan, K. 1987. "The Perils and Paradoxes of Feminist Pedagogy." *Resources for Feminist Research* 16, no. 3: 49–51.

Nelson, P. 1995. *Penny Dreadful.* St. Leonards: Random House.

Newton, E. 1948. Letter to Miss Fifi Hawthorne. Box 204, 1489, Kambala Archives.

Nobbs, A. 1987. *Kambala: The First Hundred Years 1887–1987.* Rose Bay: Kambala Centenary History Committee.

O'Malley, S. 1989. "Introduction to a CUNY Faculty Development Seminar on Balancing the Curriculum." *Radical Teacher* 27: 14–26.

Park School Community Council. 1971. "Downtown Kids Aren't Dumb: They Need a Better Program." Brief to the Management Committee of the Toronto Board of Education (November 16). *This Magazine Is about Schools* 5, no. 4: 6–35.

Poynting, S. 2000. "Ethnicizing Criminality and Criminalizing Ethnicity." In *The Other Sydney: Communities, Identities and Inequalities in Western Sydney*, edited by J. Collins and S. Poynting, 63–78. Melbourne: Common Ground Publishing.

Reakes, J. 1987. *How to Trace Your Convict Ancestors.* Sydney: Hale & Iremonger.

Repo, M. 1977. "The Fallacy of Community Control." In *Community or Class Struggle,* edited by J. Cowley, A. Kaye, M. Mayo, and M. Thompson, 47–64. London: State 1.

Riley, D. 1967. "A History of the Evers' Family." Unpublished manuscript, Parramatta, NSW (September 21).

Ritchie, J. 1988. "Come Outside and Play." *Sporting Traditions* 5, no. 1: 77–88.

Robson, L. 1994. *The Convict Settlers of Australia,* 2nd ed. Melbourne: Melbourne University Press.

Ross, P. 1990. Memorandum to all principals, "Abortion and Homosexuality" (February 2).

Ryan, E. 1986. "Women in Production in Australia." In *Australian Women: New Feminist Perspectives,* edited by N. Grieve and A. Burns, 258–272. Melbourne: Oxford University Press.

School Programs Committee. 1986. Amendment to Report No. 3 of School Programs Committee (April 23).

Spender, D. 1980. "Educational Institutions: Where Cooperation Is Called Cheating." In *Learning to Lose,* edited by D. Spender and E. Sarah, 22–31. London: Women's Press.

Stack, C. 1986. "The Culture of Gender: Women and Men of Color." *Signs* 11, no. 2: 321–324.

Steedman, C. 1982. *The Tidy House.* London: Virago.

———. 1986. *Landscape for a Good Woman.* London: Virago.

Summers, A. 1975. *Damned Whores and God's Police.* Ringwood: Penguin.

Teese, R. 1998. "Curriculum Hierarchy, Private Schooling, and the Segmentation of Australian Secondary Education, 1947–1985." *British Journal of Sociology of Education* 19, no. 3: 401–417.

Theobald, M. 1996. *Knowing Women: Origins of Women's Education in Nineteenth-Century Australia*. Cambridge: Cambridge University Press.

Thompson, B., and E. Disch. 1992. "Feminist, Anti-racist, Anti-oppression Teaching: Two White Women's Experience." *Radical Teacher* 41: 4–10.

Tronto, J. 1987. "Beyond Gender Difference to a Theory of Care." *Signs* 12, no. 4: 644–663.

University of Melbourne. 2003. Andrew Ross. *Bright Sparcs Registry* <www.asap.unimelb/edu.au/bsparcs/biogs/P000147b.htm>.

Visser, A. 1991. "Anti-homophobia Program Goes Ahead." *Xtra* (December 27): 9.

Wheatley, N. 1988. "All in the Same Boat? Sydney's Rich and Poor in the Great Depression." In *Making a Life*, edited by V. Burgmann and J. Lee, 205–225. Fitzroy: McPhee Gribble/Penguin.

Wherry, J. 2003. "Selected Parent Involvement Research." The Parent Institute <www.par-inst.com/parent/resources/research/research.php>.

Windschuttle, E., ed. 1980. *Women, Class and History: Feminist Perspectives on Australia, 1788–1978*. Melbourne: Fontana.

Wright, O. 1991. Letter to T. McCaskell and T. Gambini (January 25).

# Copyright Acknowledgments

An earlier version of Chapter 5 appeared as:
"Going Too Far? Sexual Orientation(s) in the Sex Education Curriculum." In *The Sociology of Education in Canada*, edited by L. Erwin and D. MacLennan, 277–289. Toronto: Copp Clark Pitman, 1994.

Chapter 6 includes revised versions of the following:
"The Politics of Feminist Pedagogy: Implications for Teaching Women in the Human Services Professions." In *Weaving Alliances*, edited by D. Martens, 35–46. Ottawa: Canadian Women's Studies Association, 1993.

"Commitment and Compromise: Feminist Pedagogy in the Academy." In *Feminism and Education: A Canadian Perspective*, vol. 2, edited by P. Bourne, P. Masters, N. Amin, M. Gonick, and L. Gribowski, 3–15. Toronto: Centre for Women's Studies in Education, Ontario Institute for Studies in Education, 1994.

"Tele-communication: Women's Studies through Distance Education." *Resources for Feminist Research* 20, no. 1/2 (1992): 11–12.

# Index

(Note: References to pages 1–94 deal with the Australian context, and Canadian references are located on pages 95–162.)

Abbotsleigh girls' school, 36, 46, 52, 54, 76, 87, 90
Aboriginal peoples, Australia, 13, 21, 57, 61
academic curriculum, NSW, 57, 70, 84
after-school programs, 114, 115, 116
Ainsworth, Mollie, 51, 56
Albion Street Superior Public School, 24–25
Alinsky, Saul, 103, 109
Anglican church, Anglicans, 35, 37, 43, 44, 60, 76–77, 86, 90
Australian accents, 62–64
autobiography, 2, 4, 45, 46, 75, 97

basketball (netball), 76, 91
Bell, Diane, 2, 3–4, 7, 25, 33
biology, 39, 84
Black students, 103, 128, 130, 141, 147, 148, 149, 150
boarding houses, 18–19, 29, 37, 52
British model of private education, 69, 89

Chow, Olivia, 134–136
Christianity, 56, 60–61, 76
citizen participation, 102–103, 107, 115, 126, 144
Coalition for Lesbian and Gay Rights in Ontario (CLGRO), 131
Collins, Patricia Hill, 129–130
Commonwealth Scholarships, 72, 82
competition, academic, 21, 43, 69, 79, 85–87
Connell, R.W., 44, 57, 67
convicts, convictism, 4, 10–11, 37

Conway, Jill Ker, 2, 4–5, 46–47, 52, 54, 70, 79, 89, 90
corporal punishment, 19, 21, 56, 89, 120
Cranbrook boys' school, 48, 59
curriculum councils, 118–120
Curriculum Guide on Homophobia and Sexual Orientations, 127, 135–144, 164

Dehli, Kari, 107, 112, 125, 128
discipline, in schools, 52, 60, 113, 119, 120, 124
discrimination, 102, 128, 130, 133, 136, 150, 157
distance education, 148–162
domestic science, 24
downtown Toronto schools/students, 101, 106–107, 115, 161

Eastdale secondary school, 104, 105
education, postsecondary, 39, 42, 53, 59, 72, 77, 86, 90
English as a Second Language, 101, 119
Epstein, Hilda, 71, 76, 80, 90
ethnic minorities/diversity, 57, 77, 99, 110, 112, 122, 127, 147, 150, 153, 155, 156, 165
Evers, Edwin, 14, 16, 27
Evers, Mary Kerr (McCallum), 11, 15
Evers, Samuel, 10, 11, 14–16, 26–27, 32, 38
Evers, Titus, 11–13, 37
Evers, William, 12, 14, 16
examinations, NSW schools, 25, 49, 79, 82, 84, 86

Federation of Women Teachers' Associations of Ontario (FWTAO), 131–132
feminist awakening stories, 97–98
feminist pedagogy, 4, 99, 145–162

feminists, feminism, 2–7, 45, 47, 48, 70, 78, 97, 98, 99, 129, 130, 132, 145–165
Frankland Community Council (FCC), 109, 112–126
Frankland public school, 101, 108–124
French, 24, 25, 84, 117
Frensham girls' school, 76, 87
Friedan, Betty, 97
friendship, 67, 73, 80

Gambini, Tony, 136, 139, 140
gay and lesbian issues, 127–144, 158–161
Gay and Lesbian Parents' Coalition, 139
Gill, Judith, 44–45, 70, 85, 93
Girls' Friendly Society, 30, 37–38
Greater Riverdale Organization (GRO), 109
Greek parents/children, 110, 112, 117–118, 122, 124

Hall-Dennis report, 110–111
harassment, 98, 128–130, 136, 150
Hawthorne, Fifi, 36–37, 48–93
heterosexism, 128, 133, 150, 157, 158, 165
history and geography, 65, 84
Home and School Associations, 107–108, 111–113
homophobia, 120, 127–150, 155–159, 161, 164, 165
house system, private schools, 87–88
housework, housekeeping, 3, 19, 20, 22–25, 29–41, 48, 88

immigrants, 103, 104, 156, 160, 163
individualistic worldview, 45, 93, 153
Intermediate Certificate, NSW, 49, 82, 84
Italian parents/children, 110, 117

Jackman public school, 117
Jefferson, Joan Margaret, sister, 9, 30, 32, 146
Jefferson, Margaret Irene (Evers), mother, 1, 7–42, 62–64, 69–70, 81, 163
Jefferson, William Hope, father, 9, 29–35, 40–41, 62–64, 67, 88
Jefferson, William Kerr, brother, 9, 32
Johnson, Jane, 10, 12
Johnson, Lesley, 3, 68, 97

Kambala Chronicle, 51, 60
Kambala Council, 48, 55
Kambala girls' school, 1, 35–42, 43–94, 101, 114, 163
Kambala, domestic staff, 48
Kambala, duties, 88

Kambala, morning assembly, 76, 78–79, 86, 89
Kambala, Old Girls (alumnae), 45, 48, 52, 54, 55, 58, 60, 89
Kambala, rules, 89
Kambala, school syllabus, 56
Keating, Don, 104, 109
Kyle, Noelene, 23–25, 44, 57, 83

Laneway Community School, 105–106
Latin, 24, 56, 76, 79, 84
Leaving Certificate, NSW, 47, 82, 83, 101
lesbians, lesbianism, 39, 50, 73, 74, 75, 97, 127–144, 149, 150, 156–159, 164
liaison parents, Frankland, 111–114
Lind, Loren, 105, 116, 117, 120

mathematics, 47, 51, 84
McCallum, Sarah Euphemia, 15, 18–21, 37
McCaskell, Tim, 132, 139, 140
McGregor, Craig, 57–64, 90
McOnie, Doris (Evers), 8, 10, 12, 14–15, 17, 27, 38, 163
menstruation, 17, 39, 93
methodology, 5, 108
middle class, 2, 4, 24, 31, 33, 35, 36, 40, 44, 50, 57–59, 63–64, 78, 103, 105, 106, 112, 115, 116, 130, 147, 150, 156, 161
Middleton, Sue, 5, 6, 97
Ministry of Education, Ontario, 136, 137
missionaries, 21, 61
*Molong Express*, 11, 12, 13, 27
Molong, NSW, 7, 8, 10–18, 26, 27, 28

Native parents/children, 103, 161
Nelson, Penny, 53, 58, 62, 86–87
Nobbs, Alanna, 48, 55–56, 60, 69
noblesse oblige, 60
Northern Ontario, 145, 155, 159, 161

Ontario Institute for Studies in Education, University of Toronto (OISE/UT), 98, 127, 151–162, 164
Opportunity Classes, 102, 105

parent education, 102, 108
Park public school, 35, 103–106, 110, 126
Parkway secondary school, 104–105
physical and health education teachers, 137, 140, 144
popular music/culture, 65–66
poverty, 17, 26, 102, 156

# INDEX

prefects, private schools, 80, 87, 89, 90
prejudice, 106, 138, 156
principal selection process, 118, 121–126

racism, 21, 102, 130, 132, 135, 138, 141, 149, 150, 155, 161–162
Regent Park school/community, 104
religion, 23, 33, 75–78, 84, 93, 133, 139, 164
religious accommodation, 164
reproduction, 39, 50, 57
Riley, Daphne, 10, 11, 14
Riverdale community, 109–110
Ross, Dr. Andrew, 15, 18, 137
ruling/upper class, 43, 44, 50, 57–59, 67, 83, 88, 93, 163
Ryan, Edna, 19, 20

school fees, 25, 36, 44, 54, 58, 65, 84
school principals, 50, 55, 91, 107, 109, 114, 118–121, 133
school sport, 51, 53, 54, 67, 69, 73, 79, 80, 82, 85, 87, 88, 90–92
school superintendents, 106, 120, 137, 138, 141, 142
school trustees, 106, 107, 108, 120–124, 133–135, 142, 164
school uniforms, 60, 72, 81, 89
schools, Catholic, 21, 43, 44–45, 58, 70, 89
schools, private/non-government, 1, 3, 6, 32, 35, 36, 43–93, 163
schools, public, 24, 25, 75
secretarial work, 72, 85
sewing, 19, 31, 40, 68, 119
sexism, 47, 77, 130, 138
sexual orientations, 127–144, 157, 164–165
sexuality, 16, 39, 64, 66, 97, 127–144, 145, 157, 164–165
shepherds, 12, 14, 17
Skinner, Freda, 78
Smith, John, 10, 12
social class, 36, 41, 44, 50, 57, 64–66, 107, 119, 129, 153, 165
sporting achievement, 54, 69, 87, 88, 92
Status of Women Committee, Toronto Board of Education, 127, 128, 138, 139, 140, 141, 144
Steedman, Carolyn, 2, 4, 7, 36, 70
swimming, 31, 35, 90, 92, 93
Sydney Kindergarten Teachers' College (formerly Sydney Kindergarten Training College), 52, 72, 101
Sydney, eastern suburbs, 31, 48, 50, 75, 91, 163

tennis, 40, 90, 91
Theobald, Marjorie, 1–2, 3, 7, 57, 78
Toronto Board of Education, 106–144, 164
Trefann Court mothers, 104–105, 116, 124, 126

violence against women and children, 7, 109, 128, 136, 155, 156
volunteer parents, 107–119

Wentworth, William Charles, 12, 87
Wheatley, Nadia, 48, 60
Withrow Area Residents' Association (WARA), 110
working class, 2, 4, 24, 25, 33, 37, 40–44, 57, 58–59, 63–65, 70, 103, 104, 106, 110, 112, 115, 116, 126, 150, 163

181